# High Scorer's Choice Series

# IELTS 5 Practice Tests

# General Set 2

## (Tests No. 6-10)

High Scorer's Choice Series, Book 4
**IELTS 5 Practice Tests, General Set 2 (Tests No. 6–10)**
**ISBN 9780648000013**
Copyright © 2017 Simone Braverman, Robert Nicholson.
First Edition May 2017

Available in print and digital formats
Accompanying audio recordings to be downloaded on the following webpage:
http://www.ielts-blog.com/ielts-practice-tests-downloads/

IELTS® is a registered trademark of University of Cambridge ESOL, the British Council, and IDP Education Australia, which neither sponsor nor endorse this book.

To contact the authors:
Email: simone@ielts-blog.com
Website: www.ielts-blog.com

## Acknowledgements

The authors hereby acknowledge the following websites for their contributions to this book (see the webpage below for a complete list):

www.ielts-blog.com/acknowledgements/

While every effort has been made to contact copyright holders it has not been possible to identify all sources of the material used. The authors and publisher would in such instances welcome information from copyright holders to rectify any errors or omissions

# Praise for
# High Scorer's Choice Practice Tests

*"I am a teacher from Australia. I had a Chinese friend who is studying for the exam and I used these [tests] to help him. I think the papers are very professional and useful. Many of the commercial practice papers are not culturally sensitive but this was not a problem with your tests."*
- *Margaretta from Australia*

*"I found out that your practice papers are excellent. I took my IELTS on March 11th and got an Overall Band 8 with listening - 8, reading - 9, writing - 7 and speaking - 7. I spent one month on preparation."*
- *Dr Yadana from London, UK*

*"I must tell you that the sample tests I have purchased from you have been the key to my preparation for the IELTS. Being employed full time I do not have the time to attend classes. I downloaded the material and made myself practice a few hours every 2 or 3 days for 3 weeks and was successful on my first trial. I was able to get an average of 7.5 and I was aiming at 7."*
- *Oswaldo from Venezuela*

## Finished *one* book? There's more!

### High Scorer's Choice - The Complete Series:

**Book 1**
**IELTS 5 Practice Tests, Academic Set 1 (Tests No. 1–5)**

**Book 2**
**IELTS 5 Practice Tests, General Set 1 (Tests No. 1–5)**

**Book 3**
**IELTS 5 Practice Tests, Academic Set 2 (Tests No. 6–10)**

**Book 4**
**IELTS 5 Practice Tests, General Set 2 (Tests No. 6–10)**

**Book 5**
**IELTS 5 Practice Tests, Academic Set 3 (Tests No. 11–15)**

**Book 6**
**IELTS 5 Practice Tests, General Set 3 (Tests No. 11–15)**

# CONTENTS

## Download Audio Content

In order to download the audio content please use a desktop computer (not a mobile device) with a reliable internet connection and open the following webpage in your browser:

**http://www.ielts-blog.com/ielts-practice-tests-downloads/**

Follow instructions on the webpage to save all audio files on your computer. The files are in mp3 format and you will need an audio player to listen to them (any modern computer has that type of software preinstalled).

# How to prepare for IELTS

There are two ways for you to use these practice tests for your exam preparation. You can either use them to work on your technique and strategy for each IELTS skill, or you can use them to simulate a real exam and make sure you will do well under time pressure.

### Option 1          Use practice tests to work on your IELTS skills (no time limits)

To prepare well for the IELTS exam you need to have a strategy for each sub-test (Listening, Reading, Writing and Speaking). This means knowing what actions to take, and in which order, when you receive a test paper. If you are working with the IELTS self-study book "Ace the IELTS – How to Maximize Your Score", all the necessary tips are located in the book. You need to read and then apply these tips and techniques when you are practicing on some of these tests. Don't time yourself, concentrate on learning the techniques and making sure they work for you.

If you purchased the practice tests in digital format, you will need to print out some pages, for easier learning and to be able to work in the same way as in the real test (on paper). Print the Listening questions and the Reading passages and questions. You can read the Writing and Speaking questions from your computer or mobile device, to save paper and ink. If you have the paperback format, this doesn't apply to you. Use Table of Contents on the previous page to navigate this book.

If Listening is one of your weaker skills, use transcripts while listening to recordings, when you hear words or sentences that you don't understand. Stop the recording, rewind, locate in the transcript the sentence you had a problem with, read it, and then listen to the recording again.

If Reading is hard for you, after doing the Reading test use the Reading Answer Help section of these practice tests to understand why the answers in the Answer key are correct. It will show you the exact locations of the answers in the Reading passages.

To compare your own writing to high-scoring samples go to Example Writing Answers and read them. Note the way the information is grouped and the tone (formal/informal) used in Writing Task 1, and the way an essay is organised in Writing Task 2.

To practice in Speaking, either read to yourself the Speaking test questions or get a friend to help with that. Record your answers and then listen to the recording. Note where you make long pauses while searching for the right word, pay attention to your errors and your pronunciation. Compare your own performance to that of students in sample interviews, and read their Examiner's reports.

## Option 2    Use practice tests to simulate the real test (strict time limits)

This option will require some prep work before you can start a simulated test. Print out or photocopy the blank Test Answer Sheets for Listening and Reading and prepare some ruled paper on which to write your Writing Task 1 and 2. Also, think of a way to record yourself in the Speaking sub-test. Get a watch, preferably with a timer. Allocate 3 hours of uninterrupted time.

1. Be in a quiet room, put the Listening questions in front of you and start playing the recording. Answer questions as you listen, and write your answers next to the questions in the book.

2. When the recording has finished playing, allocate 10 minutes to transfer all your Listening answers to the Listening Answer Sheet. While you are transferring the answers check for spelling or grammatical errors and if you missed an answer, write your best guess.

3. Put the Reading passages and questions in front of you and set the timer to 60 minutes. Begin reading passages and answering questions. You can write the answers next to the questions or straight on the Answer Sheet. Remember that you don't get extra time to copy answers to the Answer Sheet, and that when 60 minutes are up all your answers must be written on the Answer Sheet.

4. Put the Writing questions in front of you and set the timer to 60 minutes. Make sure you don't use more than 20 minutes for Task 1, including proofreading time, and that you don't use more than 40 minutes for Task 2, with proofreading included.

5. Put the Speaking questions in front of you and begin the interview (remember to record your answers). In Section 2 take the whole 1 minute to prepare your speech and make notes, and then try to speak for 2 minutes (set the timer before you start talking).

6. When you have finished the whole test, take some time to rest, as you may be tired and it may be hard for you to concentrate. Then check your answers in the Listening and Reading against the correct ones in the Answer key, compare your writing tasks to the Example Writing tasks and your recorded speaking to the example interview. Analyse and learn from any mistakes you may find, and especially notice any problems with time management you may have encountered.

   Remember, it is OK to make mistakes while practicing as long as you are learning from them and improving with every test you take.

   Good luck with your exam preparation!

# PRACTICE TEST 6

## LISTENING

 Download audio recordings for the test here:
http://www.ielts-blog.com/ielts-practice-tests-downloads/

### SECTION 1      *Questions 1 – 10*

**Questions 1 – 5**

*Complete the house insurance claim form below.*

*Write **NO MORE THAN THREE WORDS AND/OR A NUMBER** from the listening for each answer.*

<table>
<tr><td colspan="2" align="center">**Clover Insurance<br>Claim Form**</td></tr>
<tr><td>*Example*</td><td>*Answer*</td></tr>
<tr><td>Policy taken out:</td><td>_8 months_ ago</td></tr>
<tr><td>Policy Holders' Names:</td><td>1    **(1)** __Colin__ Hudson</td></tr>
<tr><td></td><td>2    Milly Hudson</td></tr>
<tr><td>Address:</td><td>**(2)** __15__ Battersea Avenue<br>Endford</td></tr>
<tr><td>Postcode:</td><td>EN6 9GD</td></tr>
<tr><td>Policy Number:</td><td>**(3)** __Ju 731__</td></tr>
<tr><td>Type of Policy:</td><td>**(4)** __Premium__</td></tr>
<tr><td>Police Case Number:</td><td>315 166 **(5)** __462__</td></tr>
</table>

## Questions 6 – 10

Choose **FIVE** letters, **A - J**.

What **FIVE** things from the list below will Mrs. Hudson claim on from her home insurance?

**A**     A window

**B**     A door

**C**     The house locks

**D**     Jewelry

**E**     Silver tie pin

**F**     Silver picture frame

**G**     About 500 pounds cash

**H**     A picture

**I**     An antique table

**J**     A porcelain vase

## SECTION 2    *Questions 11 - 20*

### *Questions 11 – 15*

*Below is a map of the beach near the Seaview Hotel. There are **8** locations marked (**A - H**).*
*Questions **11 - 15** list 5 locations on and near the beach. Match the locations in questions **11 - 15**
with the correct locations on the map and write the correct letter (**A - H**) next to questions **11 - 15**.*

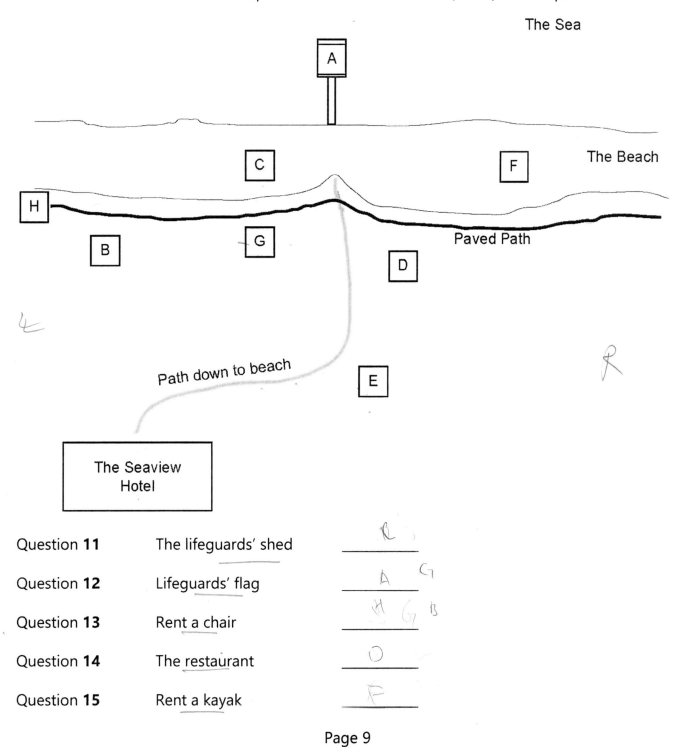

| Question **11** | The lifeguards' shed | _____ |
| Question **12** | Lifeguards' flag | _____ |
| Question **13** | Rent a chair | _____ |
| Question **14** | The restaurant | _____ |
| Question **15** | Rent a kayak | _____ |

Page 9

## Questions 16 – 20

*Answer the questions below.*

Use **NO MORE THAN THREE WORDS AND/OR A NUMBER** *from the listening for each answer.*

**16**   When will *Murder in the Library* finish?   *10 pm*

**17**   What is between the Playhouse Theatre and the Summer Showhouse?   *garage structure*

**18**   Where does the speaker recommend to watch the firework display?   *benches*

**19**   Where will the culinary festival be held?   *town center*

**20**   How does the speaker advise the listeners to go to the Comedy Club?   *bring umbrella, taxi*

## SECTION 3        *Questions 21 – 30*

### *Questions 21 – 25*

*Complete the sentences below.*

*Use **NO MORE THAN TWO WORDS** from the listening for each answer.*

**21**    Richard said he wanted to study a language from outside _____ before he went to university.

**22**    The tennis club allowed Richard to work without a _____.

**23**    Richard found the _____ of Arabic very easy.

**24**    Richard found that he improved his spoken Arabic most in _____ after work.

**25**    Richard said that the _____ of some restaurants' food was not so good.

**Questions 26 – 30**

Complete Richard's interview notes below.

Use **NO MORE THAN THREE WORDS** from the listening for each answer.

---

### Interview Notes

The two languages I will study at university will be (26) _____ and French.

The teaching will consist of the following:

| Year 1 | * School-type lessons on grammar<br>* Seminars (6 - 10 people) to discuss set readings - focus on fluency and (27) _____ |
|--------|-----------------------------------------------------------------------------------------------------------------------------------|
| Year 2 | * School-type lessons on grammar (more obscure/difficult areas)<br>* Seminars on literature and cultural topics |
| Year 3 | * Spent in two countries; 5 months each<br>* Study at university or work<br>* What is studied at a foreign university must be an (28) _____; the university has a list<br>* Student can arrange work placements themselves or the university can use its (29) _____ |
| Year 4 | * No more lessons on grammar. Replaced by seminars on language points (teachers and students can bring up topics)<br>* Lectures on literature |

Year 4 also has the final exams:

Early May     Oral exam (with native speaker teacher)

Early June    Two (30) _____ exams
              A listening exam
              Two literature exams (dependent on topics I choose)

Course grade calculated on exam performance, various course assignments and the third year dissertation.

## SECTION 4        Questions 31 – 40

### Questions 31 – 38

Complete the table below on the development of the match as described in the listening.

Write **NO MORE THAN TWO WORDS AND/OR A NUMBER** from the listening for each answer.

| INVENTOR | DATE | NOTES |
|---|---|---|
| The ability to make fire spread slowly around the world due to the natural constraints of rain and wind; it's also difficult to (31) _____ fire. | | |
| The Chinese | 5th - (32) _____ century AD | Sulphur coated sticks developed and later used throughout China. |
| Hennig Brandt | 2nd half of 17th century | Explored the (33) _____ of pure phosphorus. Very useful for later inventors. |
| Jean Chancel | 1805 | Created the 1st match, but not like today's. Sticks tipped with chemicals dipped into sulphuric acid to create fire. The fire released (34) _____ that could make users sick. This method did not become popular. |
| John Walker | 1826 | This method used (35) _____ to ignite the match in a fold of sandpaper. |
| | 1827 - 1829 | Walker's matches popularised, but lost popularity and later banned because of their (36) _____. |
| Charles Sauria | 1830's | Made the 1st match using white phosphorus. |
| | By 1850 | Effective, but the match's habit of (37) _____ led to their ban as well. |
| Johan Lundström | The late 1840's | Used red phosphorus, but on the (38) _____, not the match, which was healthier and safer. |
| | By 1858 | Lundström could manufacture 12 million match boxes a year. Became the match people use today. |

**Questions 39 and 40**

*Label the image of gas release in Lundström's safety match below.*

*Use **NO MORE THAN TWO WORDS** from the listening for each answer.*

**Gas Release in Lundström's
Safety Match**

Luminous yellow gas

Combustion products visible as a
familiar **(40)** _____ Orange flame

Hot pyrolysis gas

Harmless Charcoal

**(39)** _____ remains after
the flame burns the wooden match

# READING

## SECTION 1          *Questions 1 – 14*

### *Questions 1 – 7*

*There are seven advertisements on the next page, **A - G**.*

*Which advertisement mentions the following information?*

*Write the correct letter, **A - G**, in boxes **1 – 7** on your answer sheet.*

**1**      Bookings are not possible.

**2**      Sleeping takes place with other people in the room.

**3**      Working in the city centre is necessary.

**4**      Check the website for deals.

**5**      A representative can visit.

**6**      Guests can cook for themselves.

**7**      Dining takes place next to the water's edge.

**A**                    *Harbour View Hotel  \*\*\*\*\**

Spend a night, weekend, week or fortnight with us and experience the luxury and beauty of this newly-opened 5\* hotel. Choose from 3 separate restaurants for your lunch and dinner and work off the delicious food in our gym or one of our heated pools, or just lie on a lounger by the pool or on our private beach. All our rooms have a view of the magnificent harbour below us and you can have a cool drink on the terrace every afternoon or evening, with the same view spread out in front of you.

*Consult our website for availability, prices and special offers!*

**B**               **The Oyster** - *The city's premier fish and seafood restaurant.*

Nestling on the sea shore, The Oyster offers only locally sourced fish and seafood, freshly caught in a sustainable way and prepared by our expert chefs. Enjoy our food in our à la carte restaurant or informal bistro. Either way, you'll get an experience to remember.

*Call ahead to book, as inclement weather and private functions can affect opening hours.*

**C**

***The Golden Onion*** - Want budget food without the budget decor? The Golden Onion is famed throughout the city for its no frills and no nonsense menus. Johnny (the owner) has the philosophy to eat well without robbing people's pockets. No reservations, just turn up. Closed on Tuesdays. Student discounts for lunches and weekday dinners. 18 Station Road, Holt.

**D**     **Aloha** - discount accommodation.
Staying in the city and short on cash? The Aloha offers you dormitory style accommodation and shared bathrooms at a fraction of what a hotel would charge. A buffet breakfast is included in the rate. Book online or give us a call on 07463 465 284.

**E**

Major city centre hotel requires a smart and multi-skilled person for reception duty. Experience and the ability to speak more than one language essential. Send your CV, photo and a covering letter with your reasons why you fit this job to the personnel manager at the Grand Hotel, Holt.

**F**

**Treetops Camping** - Situated 5 miles from the city centre, Treetops offers a place for you to relax in nature away from the hustle and bustle of the city. Bring and pitch your own tent or rent one of our self-catering cabins (capacity 5). Check our website for details: www.treetops.com.

**G**        **Morgan Catering Supplies**
Whether you're a hotel or a restaurant, Morgan Catering Supplies will be able to fulfill all your food needs. Fresh and local produce is our speciality, though we also have access to all foodstuffs from around the world. Call one of our salespeople, so we can visit your premises or discuss things on the phone. 01742 657 299

**Questions 8 – 14**

Do the following statements agree with the information given in the text?

In boxes **8 – 14** on your answer sheet write:

      **TRUE**               *if the statement agrees with the information*
      **FALSE**            *if the statement contradicts the information*
      **NOT GIVEN**    *if there is no information on this*

**8**        The car boot sale is easily reached by public transport.

**9**        The car boot sale is cancelled in bad weather.

**10**     Sellers must finish and leave by 2.30 p.m.

**11**     Sellers with a lot to sell can bring a truck at extra charge.

**12**     The website provides any latest news regarding the car boot sale.

**13**     Sellers are usually happy that buyers ask lots of questions about items being sold.

**14**     Thieves sometimes operate at car boot sales.

## Hardley Heath Car Boot Sale

The Hardley Heath Car Boot Sale is one of the largest in the area. Join us on every Sunday morning of the year to buy or sell at the Hardley Heath Arena. Surrounded by beautiful terraced amphitheatres and extensive areas of secure car parking, the multi-functional and all weather Hardley Heath Arena is THE all purpose open air arena complex. The Hardley Heath Arena has easy access from different roads for drivers and the number 76 bus stops right outside.

For the uninitiated, a car boot sale is when ordinary people clear out things they don't want any more, put them in the car boot and then sell the contents to the public. It's a great way to get rid of things and make money as a seller and to find bargains if you're a buyer.

Open every Sunday, from 15th March to 15th December, rain, shine or snow!

### For Sellers

* Open for setting up from 5.00 a.m.
* £10 per car
* No lorries, please!
* Hot food and drinks available from 5.30 a.m.
* Try and be with us by 6.30 a.m.
* £15 per van
* No reservation required

Some people like to put price tags on their items, others prefer not too, so it's up to you. Not putting a price tag can make a lot of buyers engage in conversation by asking the price and once the talking's going, it's your chance to make the sale. If you think you have a valuable antique or item, get it evaluated by a professional, don't just guess at the price! Treat your stall like a shop window! You should try to reposition your items several times during the course of the day. This will create a different looking selection and buyers may well notice items they did not see before as they walk around for a second or even third time!

### For Buyers/Browsers

* Open from 7.00 a.m.
* On foot no charge
* Parking for 5000 cars (50p per car/motorbike)
* Supervised fun and games area for kids
* Hot food and drinks available all day

Remember that the early bird catches the worm! Sellers are up notoriously early, so to ensure that you get the pick of the best on each stall, get there as soon as you can. There's always the opportunity to catch up on a bit of sleep after you've captured a few bargains! If you see an item that you think you might want, sellers welcome as many questions as you feel necessary. The seller will no doubt have a better understanding of the backstory of an item, so you can get all the information you need from them rather than making assumptions. After buying an item, whilst it might be tempting to leave your purchase with the seller for safe-keeping, it's always better to keep your hands on the thing you've bought. The seller may decide to leave early, or they could also sell your item to another bidder at a higher price. Even if they give you your money back, you've lost the item that you wanted. At the same time, be careful of pickpockets in the crowds when carrying your items around. Finally, the chances are that many of the items on sale will be relatively cheap, so make sure you have plenty of small change with you.

A recent review from our website: *"Great, great, great! Would not miss it - every Sunday I am there without fail and always come away with a bargain."*

## SECTION 2          *Questions 15 – 27*

*Questions 15 – 20*

Answer the questions below.

Write **NO MORE THAN THREE WORDS** from the text for each answer.

Write your answers in boxes **15 - 20** on your answer sheet.

15      What feature of the Eastways package allows a package or letter to be tracked?

16      What is offered to silver customers if they go beyond their monthly limit?

17      How many letters can be delivered for free with Eastways' gold service?

18      What factor influences the change in Eastways' charges?

19      How should people complain about any of Eastways' services?

20      What are readers advised to find on Eastways' website?

## Eastways Courier Services

Eastways offers the most flexible and cost-effective courier service on the market today. We can pick up a package from your premises or you can drop things off at any of our centres, which are manned 24 hours a day. You can prepare and pay for any of the parcels that you want to send at your offices or at home. All you need to do is to log in to our website and fill in the package and receiver details. The fee is calculated automatically and charged to your account. You can pay by credit card if you don't have an account yet. You then just need to print out the label and stick it on the package. The bar code on the label will be scanned every time your package is moved, and in this way you can track your package 24 hours a day and know exactly where it is and what its status is.

Bronze Service

20 letters or packages per month free of charge of weight up to 20 kilograms; discounts on national and international pick-ups and deliveries when 20 letters or packages are passed.

Silver Service

50 letters or packages per month free of charge of weight up to 20 kilograms (discounts on weights over this); considerable discounts on national and international pick-ups and deliveries when 50 letters or packages are passed.

Gold Service

Unlimited monthly numbers of letters and packages of weight up to 20 kilograms (considerable discounts on weights over this); all pick-ups and deliveries free of charge for national and international deliveries.

Online Trader Service

Successful businesses that sell online require a specialised, efficient and cost-effective service. To receive a bespoke service, call 0300 654 112 to discuss your requirements with a sales executive on our team. Our service can include dedicated daily pick-ups, weekend pick-ups and specialised bulk discounts.

Please consult our sales executives for current details of our price lists. Prices vary considerably due to fuel price fluctuations and our costs and charges are updated regularly to reflect rises and drops.

Please note that we are not allowed to deliver certain goods, for instance any dangerous items or parcels with things of exceptional value. We have made a checklist of all goods that are excluded from shipment and we can supply this list on request.

*Complaints* - Of course, we will handle your parcels with the best possible care. However, it might occur that you have a complaint about a delivery. In that case, our Customer Service Agents are ready to help. Send an e-mail to our Customer Services department via the contact details listed. If our Customer Service department can't solve your inquiry, they will forward it directly to our Claims Department. This department will look into whether or not your claim is valid and qualifies for compensation.

*Check our website for recommendations from hundreds of satisfied businesses in your area.*

## Questions 21 – 27

Complete the flow chart below.

Write **NO MORE THAN THREE WORDS** from the text for each answer.

Write your answers in boxes **21 – 27** on your answer sheet.

### *My First Day at MediaWork*

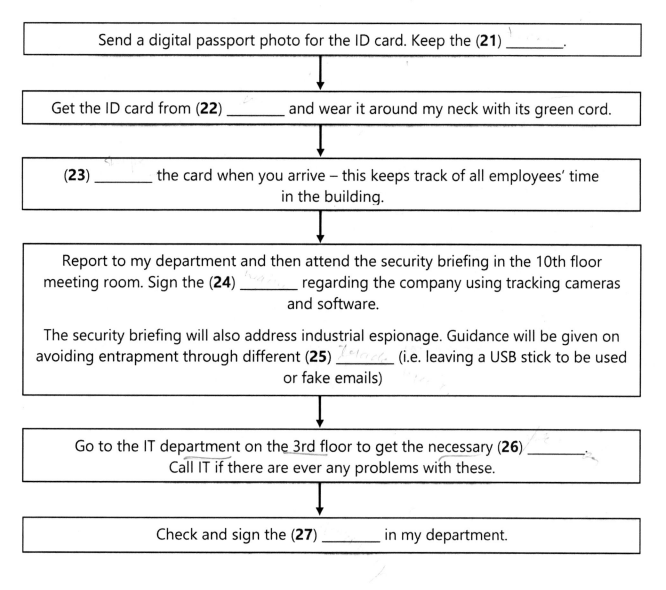

Send a digital passport photo for the ID card. Keep the (**21**) _____.

Get the ID card from (**22**) _____ and wear it around my neck with its green cord.

(**23**) _____ the card when you arrive – this keeps track of all employees' time in the building.

Report to my department and then attend the security briefing in the 10th floor meeting room. Sign the (**24**) _____ regarding the company using tracking cameras and software.

The security briefing will also address industrial espionage. Guidance will be given on avoiding entrapment through different (**25**) _____ (i.e. leaving a USB stick to be used or fake emails)

Go to the IT department on the 3rd floor to get the necessary (**26**) _____. Call IT if there are ever any problems with these.

Check and sign the (**27**) _____ in my department.

## MediaWork PLC - Security for New Staff

Welcome to your new job at MediaWork. In order to ensure your personal security and the security of the company, we ask you to read, take note of, and act on the information below.

First, we require a passport sized digital photo for your company ID card. Please email us one as soon as possible. If you have to pay for one, please retain the receipt, so that you can be reimbursed.

When you arrive for your first day at work, please go to reception. They will be expecting you and will issue you with your ID card. The card has a long green cord attached to it. Please wear the ID card around your neck at all times whilst in the company building. In this way, it's easy to spot anyone who should not be in the building.

After you receive your ID card and every time you enter or leave the company building, please swipe your card on the reader at the entrance. The reader is at chest level for people who already have the cards around their necks. The swiping of your card allows the company to track your working hours, so that they can correctly assess any overtime or flexitime that you do. It also allows the company to know who is in the building at any one time, in case there is a fire practice or emergency.

After you have reported to your department, your first day induction will begin with a security briefing. This will let you know about various security procedures that are necessary in our company. This will take place in the meeting room on the 10th floor. During it, you will be asked to endorse a waiver, allowing us to monitor your movements around the building on our CCTV system and your movements on the Internet. Our systems are designed to cover all people's movements around the building for security purposes and they are not designed to single out you or any other individual. Your security briefing will also outline procedures to do with approaches by people for information. MediaWork PLC works with a lot of large companies and our employees are privy to a lot of sensitive information. Other organisations have been known to approach our trusted employees who have access to privileged trade secrets and other valuable information and offer them money, or blackmail them into cooperation. Various social engineering techniques can also be used to gather secret information or extract credentials from employees. Random USB sticks, left in a hallway for curious employees to pick up and use, or carefully written emails that prompt clicking on a link, are only two of a large number of ways through which malware can infect our systems, giving competitors full access to sensitive data. Your security briefing will go more fully into all these threats. All our security rules are formalised into a clearly written security policy that we effectively enforce. You will be taken through this security policy and all new employees are required to sign it and acknowledge that they have read, understood and will follow what is in it.

After your security briefing, please go to the IT department on the 3rd floor. The IT people will assign you all the passwords that you will need to operate our systems. Please commit these to memory as soon as you can. If you feel that any of your passwords are compromised, let the IT department know as soon as possible, so that they can cancel them and issue new ones.

Finally, on return to your department, you will be asked to read and initial our visitors' policy. We all have visitors from time to time and your visitors must be met at reception by you, so that you can sign them in. Visitors will be issued a visitors' card, which has a bright blue cord that must be worn around their necks for easy identification.

## SECTION 3          *Questions 28 – 40*

### *Questions 28 – 34*

*The text on the following pages has 7 paragraphs (**A – G**).*

*Choose the correct heading for each paragraph from the list of headings below.*

*Write the correct number (**i – x**) in boxes **28 – 34** on your answer sheet.*

| | |
|---|---|
| **i** | A Key Ingredient |
| **ii** | Bread as an Industry |
| **iii** | South American Influences |
| **iv** | The Methods Spread |
| **v** | A Time of Change |
| **vi** | Taxes Affect Trade |
| **vii** | The Ancient Process |
| **viii** | The Essential Process |
| **ix** | New Recipes |
| **x** | Respect for a Skill and a Product |

28    Paragraph A

29    Paragraph B

30    Paragraph C

31    Paragraph D

32    Paragraph E

33    Paragraph F

34    Paragraph G

# A History of Bread

## Paragraph A

Although bread is not a staple food in all countries around the world, it is in many and in others it is of great importance. As an example, the UK bakery market is worth £3.6 billion annually and is one of the largest markets in the food industry. Total volume at present is approximately just under 4 billion units, the equivalent of almost 11 million loaves and packs sold every single day. There are three principal sectors that make up the UK baking business. The larger baking companies produce around 80 per cent of bread sold in the UK. In-store bakeries within supermarkets produce about 17 per cent and high street retail craft bakers produce the rest. In contrast to the UK, artisan bakeries still dominate the market in many mainland European countries. This allows genuine craftspeople to keep alive and indeed develop skills that have been passed on for thousands of years.

## Paragraph B

Recent evidence indicates that humans processed and consumed wild cereal grains as far back as 23,000 years ago. Archaeologists have discovered simple stone mechanisms that were used for smashing and grinding various cereals to remove the inedible outer husks and to make the resulting grain into palatable and versatile food. As humans evolved, they mixed the resulting cracked and ground grains with water to create a variety of foods from thin gruel, to a stiffer porridge. By simply leaving the paste to dry out in the sun, a bread-like crust would be formed. This early bread was particularly successful, when wild yeast from the air combined with the flour and water. The early Egyptians were curious about the bread 'rising' and attempted to isolate the yeast, so that they could introduce it directly into their bread. Bakers experimented with leavened doughs and through these experiments Egyptians were the first to uncover the secret of yeast usage. Hence, the future of bread was assured.

## Paragraph C

As travellers took bread-making techniques and moved out from Egyptian lands, the art began spreading to all parts of Europe. A key civilisation was the Romans, who took their advanced bread techniques around Europe with them. The Romans preferred whiter bread, which was possible with the milling processes that they had refined. This led to white bread being perceived as the most valuable bread of them all, a preference that seems to have stuck with many people. The Romans also invented the first mechanical dough-mixer, powered by horses and donkeys.

## Paragraph D

Both simple, yet elusive, the art of controlling the various ingredients and developing the skills required to turn grain and water into palatable bread, gave status to individuals and societies for thousands of years. The use of barley and wheat led man to live in communities and made the trade of baker one of the oldest crafts in the world. From the very beginning, people saw the benefits of eating bread. Bread is a staple part of a healthy eating pattern as it is low in fat and one of the best sources of fibre. It is made up of energy-providing carbohydrates, protein, vitamins and minerals. Bread can also provide a significant amount of people's daily requirements of calcium.

## Paragraph E

Before the Industrial Revolution, millers used windmills and watermills, depending on their locations, to turn the machinery that would grind wheat to flour. The Industrial Revolution really moved the process of bread making forwards. The first commercially successful engine did not appear until 1712, but it wasn't until the invention of the Boulton & Watt steam engine in 1786 that the process was advanced and refined. The first mill in London using the steam engine was so large and efficient that in one year it could produce more flour than the rest of the mills in London put together. In conjunction with steam power, a Swiss engineer in 1874 invented a new type of mill. He designed rollers made of steel that operated one above the other. It was called the reduction roller-milling system, and these machines soon became accepted all over Europe.

## Paragraph F

Since Egyptian times, yeast has been an essential part of bread making around the world, but yeast was not really understood properly until the 19th century. It was only with the invention of the microscope, followed by the pioneering scientific work of Louis Pasteur in the late 1860's, that yeast was identified as a living organism and the agent responsible for dough leavening. Shortly following these discoveries, it became possible to isolate yeast in pure culture form. With this newfound knowledge, the stage was set for commercial production of baker's yeast and this began around the turn of the 20th century. Since that time, bakers, scientists and yeast manufacturers have been working to find and produce pure strains of yeast that meet the exacting and specialised needs of the baking industry.

## Paragraph G

The basics of any bread dough are flour, water, and of course, yeast. As soon as these ingredients are stirred together, enzymes in the yeast and the flour cause large starch molecules to break down into simple sugars. The yeast metabolises these simple sugars and exudes a fluid that releases carbon dioxide into the dough's minute cells. As more and more tiny cells are filled, the dough rises and leavened bread is the result.

Glossary

to leaven – the process of adding yeast to bread and allowing it to 'rise'

## Questions 35 – 38

Do the following statements agree with the views of the writer of the text?

In boxes **35 - 38** on your answer sheet write:

| | |
|---|---|
| **YES** | if the statement agrees with the writer's views |
| **NO** | if the statement doesn't agree with the writer's views |
| **NOT GIVEN** | if it is impossible to say what the writer thinks about this |

**35**     Few European countries today favour the craft style bread made by independent bakeries.

**36**     The first leavening effects were done accidentally.

**37**     An ancient culture is responsible for one of today's favoured types of bread.

**38**     Pasteur's work in the 19th century allowed bread to be manufactured more cheaply.

## Questions 39 and 40

Label the diagram below.

Write **NO MORE THAN TWO WORDS** from the text for each answer.

Write your answers in boxes **39 and 40** on your answer sheet.

**The Leavening
Process**

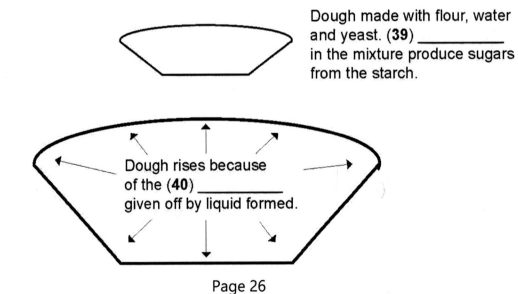

Dough made with flour, water and yeast. **(39)** _____ in the mixture produce sugars from the starch.

Dough rises because of the **(40)** _____ given off by liquid formed.

# WRITING

## WRITING TASK 1

*You should spend about 20 minutes on this task.*

**You have seen an advertisement for an evening course to study a foreign language.**

**Write a letter to the institution offering the course. In your letter,**

- **ask for details of the course**
- **ask if the course teachers are qualified native speakers**
- **request that the institution sends you their brochure**

*You should write at least 150 words.*

*You do **NOT** need to write any addresses. Begin your letter as follows:*

**Dear Sir / Madam,**

## WRITING TASK 2

*You should spend about 40 minutes on this task.*

*Write about the following topic:*

**Do you feel that it is a good idea for governments to place a restriction on the number of children a family can have in order to control rising population numbers?**

*Give reasons for your answer and include any relevant examples from your knowledge or experience.*

*You should write at least 250 words.*

# SPEAKING

## SECTION 1

- Can you describe to me the room where you sleep?
- How much sleep do you need every night?
- Do you like to sleep during the day? (Why/Why not?)

Topic 1    Fashion
- Are you a fashionable person?
- What clothing fashions are popular in your country?
- Do you think that the fashion industry involves too much money for what it is?
- Can people be fashionable without spending too much money?

Topic 2    Mobile Phones
- When did you get your first mobile phone?
- Do you feel that they are too common in today's society?
- Where would be good places to ban the use of mobile phones?
- How can we stop young people using their mobile phones so much?

## SECTION 2

> Describe an advertisement that is particularly memorable for you.
> You should say:
>     what this advertisement is for   *one of that for Jewellery brand*
>     when you saw it   *in childhood gold*
>     what is in the advertisement   *mother & son*
> and explain why this advertisement is so memorable for you.   *It beautifully conveys*

## SECTION 3

Topic 1    The Advertising Industry
- Do you feel that you are affected by advertising? (Why/Why not?)
- What makes an advertisement memorable?
- Should advertising be allowed to target children?
- How do you think the advertising industry has changed during your lifetime?

Topic 2    Advertising and the Tobacco Industry
- How do you feel about tobacco products being advertised in the media?
- What do you think about the claim that tobacco advertising just persuades people to change brands rather than persuading them actually to take up smoking?
- How can the packaging of cigarettes encourage/discourage people to start or continue smoking?
- Should tobacco advertisers and tobacco companies be at least partially responsible for financing the treatment of smoking-related diseases?

# PRACTICE TEST 7

## LISTENING

 Download audio recordings for the test here:
http://www.ielts-blog.com/ielts-practice-tests-downloads/

**SECTION 1**    *Questions 1 – 10*

*Questions 1 – 5*

*Circle the correct letters **A - C**.*

> **Example**
>
> Pete went on holiday to
> **A**    the UK.
> **B**    the United States.
> **(C)**    Canada.

1    Pete missed his flight because
　　**A**    he went to the wrong airport.
　　**(B)**    he was caught in a traffic jam.
　　**C**    the road to the airport was closed.

2    Pete managed to get a flight
　　**A**    for free two days later.
　　**B**    the next day, but not free of charge.
　　**(C)**    for free the next day.

3    Pete's airline paid for
　　**(A)**    a hotel for the night.
　　**(B)**    some food while he waited.
　　**C**    a return taxi to his friend's house.

4    Pete spent most of his flight
　　**(A)**    talking.
　　**B**    reading.
　　**C**    sleeping.

5    Pete's final problem in Toronto was that
　　**(A)**    the airline lost his bags.
　　**B**    he waited for hours in immigration.
　　**C**    he had forgotten his warm coat.

Page 29

## Questions 6 – 10

Choose **FIVE** letters, **A - J**.

What **FIVE** things from the list below did Pete do during his visit to Toronto?

**A**    Pete went up the CN Tower

**B**    Pete visited the Exhibition at Fort York

**C**    Pete went to the Royal Ontario Museum

**D**    Pete visited the Air and Space Museum

**E**    Pete visited the Art Gallery of Toronto

**F**    Pete watched a hockey game

**G**    Pete visited the Hockey Hall of Fame

**H**    Pete watched a football game

**I**    Pete watched a baseball game

**J**    Pete watched a basketball game

## SECTION 2          Questions 11 - 20

### Questions 11 – 15

*Complete the summary of the first part of the talk on Sunnyside Farm.*

*Write **NO MORE THAN THREE WORDS** for each answer.*

> **A History of Sunnyside Farm**
>
> The start of the Open Day introductory talk is on the history of the Wilson family at Sunnyside Farm. From around 1900, the farm was arable, producing (**11**) _____ for the local area. After World War 1, the farm took the unusual step of producing meat for (**12**) _____. The farm was closed in World War 2, but re-opened afterwards. In the early 1970's, the farm produced milk. The switch to milk was a financial risk, but successful. Around 10 years ago, the farm had too much (**13**) _____ from big companies. Mr. and Mrs. Wilson switched to farm tourism, getting the idea after a (**14**) _____. This project is mainly aimed at (**15**) _____.

### Questions 16 – 20

*Match the Sunnyside Farm activities (questions **16 - 20**) with their locations (**A - F**).*

*Write the correct letter (**A - F**) next to questions **16 - 20**.*

| **ACTIVITY** | | **LOCATION** | |
|---|---|---|---|
| 16 | See museum of dairy farming | **A** | The East Barn |
| 17 | Milk cows | **B** | The South Field |
| 18 | Feed lambs | **C** | The Old Dairy |
| 19 | Watch sheepdogs in action | **D** | The North Field |
| 20 | See the future campsite location | **E** | The West Stable |
| | | **F** | The West Field |

## SECTION 3    *Questions 21 – 30*

### *Questions 21 – 25*

*Choose the correct letter **A, B, or C**.*

**21**    What was the main objection to Dominic's training?

- ~~**A**~~    The expense
- **B**    He would miss a meeting
- **C**    He would have to travel too far

**22**    When do Grace and Dominic arrange to meet?

- **A**    An hour before work on Monday
- **B**    After work on Friday
- **C**    Thursday morning

**23**    Why will Grace need her computer at her meeting with Dominic?

- **A**    To look at the new designs
- **B**    To view the model Dominic has made
- **C**    To have the sales forecasts on it

**24**    How will Dominic pay for his hotel?

- **A**    He will pay himself and claim the money back
- **B**    He will use the company credit card
- **C**    The company will give him cash in advance

**25**    How will Dominic travel to his training?

- **A**    By plane
- **B**    By car
- **C**    By train

## Questions 26 – 28

Below is a plan of the Green Bay Business Park with **15** locations marked (**A - O**).
Questions **26 - 28** list **3** locations in and next to the conference reception room.
Match the locations in questions **26 - 28** with the correct locations on the map and
write the correct letter (**A - O**) next to questions **26 - 28**.

26      The GPS Center

27      Forward Thinking

28      Recycling Center

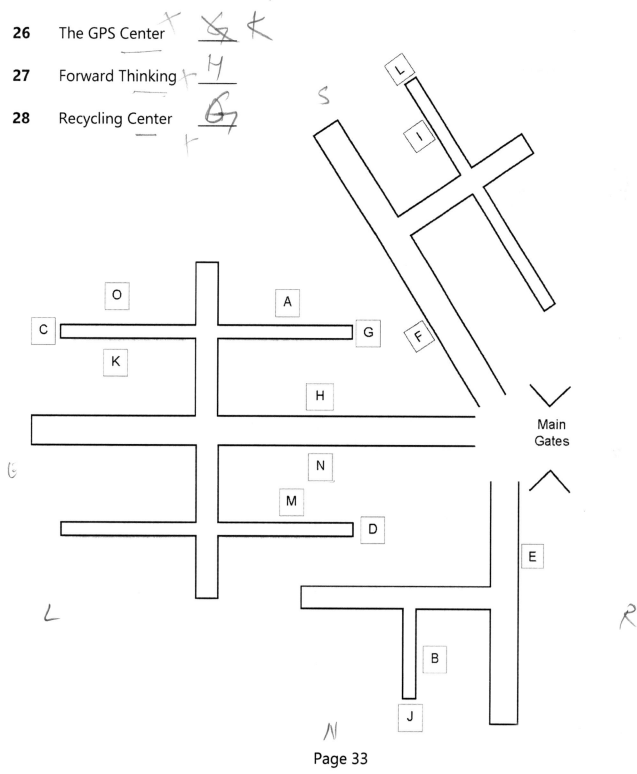

## Questions 29 and 30

*Complete the sentences below.*

*Use **NO MORE THAN TWO WORDS** from the listening for each answer.*

29    Dominic only needs to take the _____ with him to identify himself.

30    Forward Thinking will give Dominic a _____ so that he can use the internet during the training day.

## SECTION 4        *Questions 31 – 40*

### *Questions 31 – 40*

*Complete the notes below.*

*Use **NO MORE THAN THREE WORDS** from the listening for each answer.*

---

**Childhood Obesity & Sugary Drinks**

Over last 30 years, US obesity rates doubled for ages 2 to 5 and tripled for ages 6 to 11.

**(31)** ____social____ and environmental pressures often to blame. Sugary drinks that have no or very small nutritional value are widely available. These drinks include soft drinks, sports drinks, fruit drinks, flavoured teas and coffees, and energy drinks.

Sugary Drink Facts and Statistics

* American consumption of soda doubled over last 25 years.
* The average American drinks 1.6 cans of soda a day (makes 500 annually).
* **(32)** _soda children_ drink even more soda than the average.
* Soda's are 13% of teenage calorie intake.
* Soda has taken over from milk as most popular young person's drink.
* Recent studies proves link between sweet drinks and teenage obesity (some studies have conflicting results.
* Sweet drinks also encourage teeth problems and weak **(33)** ___bones___.

Sugary Drinks and Caffeine

Sugary drinks can include around 10 grams of caffeine per ounce. The recommended dose for children is well under 100 grams a day. Excess caffeine in children can lead to **(34)** _____, sleep problems and agitation. It can also lead to high blood pressure and headaches. _hyperactive_

Energy Drinks and Alcohol

Young people can mix alcohol and energy drinks. Leads to more alcohol drunk and very high **(35)** _sugar_ intake from the energy drinks and alcohol.

Possible Action

Replace sugary drinks with water or **(36)** _____.  _low-fat milk_
Monitor children and ask schools to remove **(37)** _machines_ selling sugary drinks.
Observe **(38)** _sugar levels_ when dealing with kids - no treats can lead to binge eating/drinking.
Parental **(39)** _role model_ important - children base their actions on their parents' habits. _guidance_

Conclusion

Parents should control their children's sugary drink intake and without obsession. Children should learn to love water and this will help their future health and weight. The answer therefore to developing healthy behaviour in children will be **(40)** _key_.

---

# READING

## SECTION 1          *Questions 1 – 14*

### *Questions 1 – 6*

*There are 6 advertisements, **A – F**, on the next page.*

*Which advertisement mentions the following information?*

*Write the correct letter, **A - F**, in boxes **1 – 6** on your answer sheet.*

1      This advertisement says there are cheaper prices if reservations are made online.

2      This advertisement says clients can pay in installments.

3      This advertisement says their employees' work is covered by insurance.

4      This advertisement says their service will deal with women more quickly.

5      This advertisement says they have international experience.

6      This advertisement says a zero-cost car is provided as part of their service.

## A
### Archer Insurance
### Low Cost Quality Car Insurance

*Give yourself peace of mind - get insurance that is worth having, but will not break the bank.*

* All motor histories considered
* Monthly payment options
* Young drivers welcome
* Free courtesy car included during repairs

* No claims bonus available
* Legal protection cover included
* Breakdown cover included
* 24-hour claims service

**Call Freefone 08008 777 111**

## B
### County Car Rentals

All vehicle types from economy cars to SUV's and vans.
Special deals are available for long rentals.
Discounts available if booked on our website.

Reservations and Emergencies: 07524 651 878
www.countycarrentals.com

## C   Perfection Car Valeting

* Fleet + contract work available
* Competitive pricing
* Cleaners fully insured
* We come to you service

Find all our contact details online
on our website @:
www.perfectioncarvaleting.com

## D
### Stanford Breakdown Services

Breaking down in your car can be a frustrating and potentially dangerous situation. Our country-wide network guarantees to get to you within 60 minutes of your call, with a female priority service in action. One modest payment will cover you and your car with our standard service and upgrades are available that include transport home, hotel accommodation and extra family cars.

*Call today to take advantage of our award-winning service.*
www.stanford.com - 08001 333 444

## E
### Williamson Motors
#### 45 Beach Parade, JU8 9UT

We are stockists of a large range of used cars. All our sales are guaranteed for one year following purchase with free servicing for two years. Buying a used car can be stressful - our salespeople provide a professional and pressure-free situation, where you will be comfortable throughout the whole sales process.

We buy as well as sell - call us today for a quote for your car: 07770 756 284.

## F

### John Hopkins - *Professional Restorer*

For over 30 years, I have been restoring classic cars for clients around the world. I can provide a perfect service covering mechanics, upholstery, bodywork and electrics. This is naturally a bespoke service, so email me today to arrange an appointment.

johnhopkins@classiccars.com

## Questions 7 – 14

Complete the summary below.

Write **NO MORE THAN THREE WORDS AND/OR A NUMBER** from the text for each answer.

Write your answers in boxes **7 - 14** on your answer sheet.

---

### Complaining about your Energy Supplier

It's not common to have to complain about an energy supplier. Before (**7**) _____ begins, contact the supplier and try to resolve the issue. The Citizens Advice Consumer Service can sometimes assist with this. Companies all have obligatory (**8**) _____ to deal with dissatisfied customers and should resolve the problem quickly. You can refer the problem to the OSE if you're not satisfied after (**9**) _____. The OSE can direct the supplier to complete certain action and its orders are (**10**) _____ for the company. Energy suppliers can also be changed, but careful research should be conducted on (**11**) _____ charged, offers and service to find the best deal. People should study various features and maybe use (**12**) _____, which can present unbiased information. The easy changing process begins with contacting the new supplier, who will require various information. They will do the rest and mail you a (**13**) _____. Most required information is found on your existing bill. Changing suppliers usually takes 17 days. There is a 14-day cooling-off period, but changing one's mind after this may incur a (**14**) _____.

---

## Complaining about / Changing your Energy Supplier

Energy suppliers in this country are generally very efficient. People only hear about the horror stories that are the exception and not the rule. Sometimes, however, you may have cause to complain to or about the company that supplies your energy.

Before starting any formal action, you should contact the energy company directly. The phone number and website will be on your energy bill. You can make a complaint by email, in writing or on the phone. Explain to the energy company what the problem is and what you want them to do about it. The Citizens Advice Consumer Service can help you through the process if you can't find the energy company's details or need support. They will give you information and advice, and lend you their expertise if you need it.

All companies are required to deal proactively with complaints from domestic consumers and they all have mandatory complaints procedures detailing how they do this. The energy company should respond and try to resolve your complaint. You then need to decide if you think their response is reasonable and will solve the problem you have.

The Ombudsman Services in charge of Energy (OSE) can investigate if the complaint hasn't been resolved to your satisfaction at the end of eight weeks. The OSE is the free independent scheme set up to investigate complaints from domestic consumers that the energy company cannot resolve. The OSE can require the company to correct the problem, apologise, explain what happened, and make a financial award. Its decisions are binding on the energy company, but not the consumer.

Another action you can take if you're not satisfied with your energy supplier is to change the supplier. If you do decide to change, make sure you compare energy tariffs and deals regularly, as this can help you make sure you're getting the best gas or electricity supply for your usage and the best service offer. Doing this can clearly highlight how much you could cut your bills by switching supplier. You may want to consider a number of factors when comparing suppliers and tariffs – from cheaper rates and customer satisfaction scores, to green energy tariffs or contracts with no exit fee, or even offers particular to your type of meter. There are a number of price comparison websites available at the present time and these can offer disinterested and simple sources of advice.

If you've never compared energy tariffs or switched gas or electricity supplier, it may seem a daunting process. But it's actually quite simple. Contact the new supplier and after you agree on your new energy offer, they'll start the process, notifying your current supplier of the switch. You will agree over the phone and the contract will arrive in the post. When speaking to the new supplier, you will have to give them: your postcode, the name of current supplier, the name of the energy offer you're currently on and how much you spend on gas and electricity (you can find this information on a recent bill), an up-to-date meter reading, your bank details if you will be paying by direct debit, your Meter Point Access Number (or 'MPAN') and Meter Point Reference Number (or 'MPRN'). You can also find these on a recent bill. Switching supplier can take up to twenty-one days. In most cases, it's around seventeen days. Your new supplier will confirm the date you'll be switched. You'll have fourteen days to cancel a switch from the date you start a contract with a new supplier. After this timeframe, there may be a penalty to exit depending on what has been agreed upon.

## SECTION 2        *Questions 15 – 27*

### *Questions 15 – 21*

*There is some advice on customer service, **A – F,** on the next page.*

*Which section of advice mentions the following information?*

*Write the correct letter, **A - F**, in boxes **15 - 21** on your answer sheet.*

**15**    Don't take a phone call in front of customers.

**16**    Smile when you see customers.

**17**    Never use bad language if customers might hear you.

**18**    Don't take customer rudeness personally.

**19**    Don't chat for too long with customers.

**20**    Address people in an appropriate way.

**21**    Make sure customers don't leave without the things they've paid for.

## Customer Service Advice

Everyone enjoys great customer service, whether you are in a shop or a restaurant. Good customer service creates repeat business, happier employees and better profitability.

### A        Welcome Customers Correctly

It's usually fine to be less formal with younger people, but older customers often don't appreciate being called "you guys" or similar. Use your common sense, and be polite. Remember, no one objects to being called "sir" or "madam"!

### B        Use Positive Body Language and Verbal Language

Customers don't want their day affected by your bad day! Look as though you're happy that the customer has come into your shop or restaurant and look as though you want to serve him/her. Positive language is a great way to avoid accidental conflicts sprung from miscommunication. While the change is subtle, it facilitates finding a solution. When the outcome takes center stage, it reduces the odds that customers will be upset.

### C        Strategies for When Things Get Busy

There's always a time when there are lots of people to deal with at the same time. Everyone expects at some time to be kept waiting, but if they see people trying to get them served, they'll be happier. Here are some tips: speak to the waiting customers and tell them you're trying to get to them. Try and get extra help to deal with the waiting customers. Don't answer the phone when there are waiting customers. Don't allow a talkative customer to take up too much of your time when others are waiting. Apologise to customers who have waited.

### D        Stay Calm when Dealing with Angry Customers

Sometimes you'll have to deal with someone with a bad attitude. Stay calm, don't take anything to heart and be polite, no matter what the customer says. Sometimes the customer will be right, so listen carefully, be sympathetic and apologise with genuine feeling. Often this approach will calm the customer down. If you start to get abuse, just ask your manager to take over. If you can, take a short break afterwards and remind yourself it's not your fault. Allow yourself to calm down - you'll probably be angry inside!

### E        End the Experience Well

Before the customer leaves, make sure he/she has the correct change, check the goods when you're packing them to make sure they have what they paid for and that everything is the right size and undamaged. The ability to close improves every single interaction. This is not closing a sale, it's closing the conversation with a customer. Your willingness to correctly close a conversation shows the customer three important things: you care about getting it right, you're willing to keep going until you get it right and the customer is the one who determines what "right" is.

### F        Create a Professional Atmosphere

Dress smartly with ironed clothes, make sure your hair is tidy, be clean shaven (if you're a man), have clean hands, eat or drink in your break room, never swear and don't talk about customers in front of other customers.

**Questions 22 – 27**

Complete the flow chart below.

Write **NO MORE THAN TWO WORDS** from the text for each answer.

Write your answers in boxes **22 – 27** on your answer sheet.

### *The Recruitment Process*

**1. Plan the Vacancy**        A resignation, new business or planned (**22**) _____ may create the need for a new worker. A selection committee (min. 3 or 4 people) will create a job description, maybe using the previous one as a basis.

**2. Advertising and Applications**        The vacancy will be advertised or a (**23**) _____ may be consulted. Applications will be vetted. An interview short list will be made and unsuccessful applicants can be contacted with an (**24**) _____. Interviewees will be contacted with some brief information.

**3. Interviews and Assessment**        The selection committee will conduct the interviews, using questions that will test candidates' (**25**) _____. The selection committee will choose the best candidate or will opt for a second interview with max. 3 interviewees before choosing the best candidate and a (**26**) _____.

**4. Check References and Offer Job**        It is essential to check the candidate's claims before a job offer is made.

**5. Review Recruited Employees**        Review new employees after three months and then annually. Base review on the job description initially used, get input from both sides and emphasise only the employee's performance. Set the next review's date and complete a (**27**) _____.

# The Recruitment Process

## 1      Plan the Vacancy

The first step in the recruitment process is to decide if your organisation needs a new employee. The need might come from someone leaving the company or increased business activity or scheduled expansion. If it's decided a new employee is needed, a selection committee should be formed. This should be made up of three or four people, at least two of whom should be from the prospective employee's future department, so that they will know about what the job will entail. The selection committee should create a job description for the vacancy. If the vacancy is for someone who has left, the previous job description would be a good starting point.

## 2      Advertising and Applications

The advertisement for the vacancy needs to be posted in appropriate places. A headhunter firm might be used if the vacancy warrants it. Applications will be received and should be reviewed by the selection committee. The committee should create a short list and contact unsuccessful applicants. A short email will suffice. Applicants on the short list should be contacted and invited to interview. Applicants will need to know when and where the interview will be and who it will be with. Some basic guidelines can often be appreciated.

## 3      Interviews and Assessment

The interviews should be conducted by the selection committee. They should have questions and/or tasks ready. Although questions will normally be related to the job description, the committee may want to include various questions that stretch and surprise the candidate to test his/her suitability. The selection committee will assess the interviewees and either choose a successful candidate or make a second short list for a second interview. The second interviews will usually be for a maximum of three candidates. Questions will normally relate to the issues that stopped an outright selection in the assessment stage. The selection committee will assess the second interviewees and choose a successful candidate and a back-up in case the job offer is refused.

## 4      Check References and Offer Job

This is an essential part of the process to ensure that everything the successful candidate has said is true. When the selection committee is satisfied, the job offer can be made.

## 5      Review Recruited Employees

It's important to review the performance of any new employee. It's recommended that there be an initial review after three months employment and then yearly after that. The initial review should be based on how the employer and employee have reviewed performance in light of the job description that was used to hire the employee. Both the employee and employer should be allowed to give input; it's most helpful if the employee does this first. The focus of the review should be solely on performance and not personality, behaviour or attitude. Good performance should be acknowledged and a plan should be created to deal with any problems. A date should be set for the next review in approximately one year's time and finally a report should be written for the appropriate managers, the human resources department and for the employee's file.

## SECTION 3        *Questions 28 – 40*

### *Questions 28 – 33*

*The text on the following pages has 6 paragraphs (**A – F**).*

*Choose the correct heading for each paragraph from the list of headings below.*

*Write the correct number (**i – ix**) in boxes **28 – 33** on your answer sheet.*

| | |
|---|---|
| i | Early Watch Manufacturing |
| ii | Increased Investment |
| iii | Early Methods of Measuring Time |
| iv | Twentieth-Century Innovations |
| v | Watchmaking Beyond Time and Technology |
| vi | The First Clocks |
| vii | Industry Competition |
| viii | The New Industry Leader |
| ix | From Early Watches To Now |

28    Paragraph A

29    Paragraph B

30    Paragraph C

31    Paragraph D

32    Paragraph E

33    Paragraph F

# A History of the Watch

## Paragraph A

The first dated evidence of a timepiece is a fragment of a Chinese sundial from circa 1500 BC, which suggests there were rudimentary attempts to keep time during this period. Later, wealthy Romans were known to carry around pocket-sized sundials, though these cannot be regarded as predecessors of the modern watch. It would take developments in measuring hours without the sun, such as water clocks, sand glasses, and candles uniformly burning away the hours to begin to measure time in the increments understood today. All of these ways for tracking time were utilised in the East, particularly in China during the Middle Ages. However, despite its more advanced culture, it appears that China had less use for the kind of accurate timekeeping that came to rule the West, because of their unique understanding of the Earth's rhythms and their different relationship with nature. In continental Europe, even though sundials received enormous attention by the Greek and Roman scientists, they remained sparsely used after the fall of Roman Empire. This situation only changed with the arrival of the Renaissance and the expansion of science, manufacture, and commerce.

## Paragraph B

After new knowledge of mechanical clocks from China and Islamic lands came to Europe, the art of mechanical clock making slowly started to spread. The original mechanical clock probably emerged out of monasteries, developed by monks as alarm mechanisms to ring the bells according to the regular and regimented hours of their rituals. Once the twenty-four equal-hour day was developed, the chiming of the bells gradually fell in line with the clock. Early clocks, both large tower as well as turret clocks and the smaller models that they were based on, were propelled by weight mechanisms. By the fifteenth century, however, the mainspring was developed, employing the stored power of a tightly coiled spring. This was soon followed by a device called the fusee, which equalised the momentum of a spring as it uncoiled. Smaller versions of this mechanism led to the invention of the watch.

## Paragraph C

The first watches were bulky and ornate and, like the early spring-powered clocks, kept time with only an hour hand, though still rather imprecisely due to errors from friction. Even though these early watches were hard to make, imprecise and easy to break, they created the basis for all future watches and enabled spreading of watchmaking industry across the world. These watches were therefore made in many places around the world, but initial dominance in the watch industry was by the British. The British factory systems emerging out of the industrial revolution and the development of the railroad combined to give birth to a strong and profitable business. The small-scale creation of watches in the early eighteenth century was a dual system of production that combined craftspeople in the metalworking industry putting out product from their workshops to be acquired and assembled in factory systems. The strategy, however, proved to be short-lived in light of more integrated approaches to watch assembly. This, poor transportation and communication among participants in the British watch industry led to them losing their market dominance.

**Paragraph D**

The defining factor of last century's technological evolution in watchmaking was precision. Watches have always evolved with respect to trends in fashion, but the mechanics of the standard spring-powered device itself had undergone few changes in three hundred years, until the advent of electronics in the middle of the twentieth century. Since precision in watchmaking was the driving force behind advances in technology, it is easy to understand how an accurate watch that could be made inexpensively would come to dominate the market. Gradually, improvements in battery technology, the miniaturisation of batteries, additional components combined with quartz technology and integrated circuit technology combined to produce the most accurate timepieces ever assembled. This accuracy has increased now that atomic watches can define a second as an exact number of oscillations of a cesium atom. So, modern metallurgy and industrial manufacture have enabled watches to become available to everyone and computer controlled digital watches have become ever present.

**Paragraph E**

The Japanese correctly identified quartz analog as the future of watchmaking and were particularly adept at developing it. Building upon early knowledge gained in part from American manufacturing, they developed large vertically integrated factories for their watchmaking companies. These firms quickly controlled their protected domestic market and built solid foundations in manufacturing based in Hong Kong that have helped them prosper until they dominated internationally. All the major watch producers utilised Hong Kong as a cheap source of labour for assembling products as well as purchasing components for watches, but the Japanese were the best at controlling their distribution channels.

**Paragraph F**

Watches are not limited to mere time keeping and the measurement of seconds, minutes, and hours are potentially only one function of a watch. Anything else has come to be called "complications" in watchmaking. As an example, perpetual calendars have been built into watches for more than two centuries. Such calendars have included everything from days and months to phases of the moon and adjustments for leap years. Modern manufacturing innovation, especially inexpensive batteries and microchips, allow for such "minor" complications in even cheaper watches. Meanwhile, time continues to be measured in increasingly precise manners, and so the evolution of the personal timepiece seems destined to continue into eternity.

## Questions 34 – 37

*Do the following statements agree with the information given in the text?*

*In boxes 34 – 37 on your answer sheet write:*

> **TRUE**          *if the statement agrees with the information*
> **FALSE**         *if the statement contradicts the information*
> **NOT GIVEN**  *if there is no information on this*

**34**     China in the Middle Ages did not share the West's obsession with precise time.

**35**     Religious worship times probably led to the development of the first mechanical clock.

**36**     Friction was used in early watches to help with accuracy.

**37**     The early British watch industry exported their product around the world.

## Questions 38 – 40

*Complete each sentence with the correct ending (**A - F**) below.*

*Write the correct letter (**A - F**) in answer boxes **38 - 40** your answer sheet.*

**38**     Bad business infrastructure

**39**     Developments in batteries and their size, along with other technological advances,

**40**     Effectively managing supply and delivery

**A**     made one entrepreneur a millionaire.

**B**     led to the British losing their early control of watch trading.

**C**     allowed unprecedented economies of scale.

**D**     led to the most precise watches being developed.

**E**     proved to be a competitive advantage of Japanese companies.

**F**     led to a modern set of factories being built.

# WRITING

## WRITING TASK 1

*You should spend about 20 minutes on this task.*

**You are the manager of a restaurant that has received a letter of complaint about poor service from a member of your staff.**

**Write a letter of apology to the person who has complained. In your letter,**

- **say how sorry you are that the person has had a poor experience**
- **explain what action has been taken against the staff member**
- **offer a free meal for four people at the restaurant as a gesture of goodwill**

*You should write at least 150 words.*

*You do **NOT** need to write any addresses. Begin your letter as follows:*

***Dear Mr. Smith,***

## WRITING TASK 2

*You should spend about 40 minutes on this task.*

*Write about the following topic:*

**Some of today's schools insist that all students have their own laptop computer in class to assist in their education.**

**Do you feel that this would be an advantage to students' education or would it be an unnecessary complication?**

*Give reasons for your answer and include any relevant examples from your knowledge or experience.*

*You should write at least 250 words.*

# SPEAKING

## SECTION 1

- Can you describe the street you live in?
- What kinds of things can make a good neighbourhood?
- What things are important in a neighbourhood for bringing up children?

Topic 1        Older People
- At what age do people retire in your country?
- What are some of the things in your country that retired people like to do with their spare time?
- Does your country have specialised retirement homes for the elderly?
- How does the government in your country support older people?

Topic 2        Family
- Do you get on with all your family?
- What do you think are more important, friends or family?
- Do you think it's important for married people to have children? (Why/Why not?)
- How are family decisions made in your family?

## SECTION 2

Describe the first computer you owned.
You should say:
>        what kind of computer it was
>        when you got it
>        what types of things you used it for
and explain how using a computer changed your life in any way.

## SECTION 3

Topic 1        Computers
- Do you often use a computer?
- How have people's attitudes changed towards computers over the years in your country?
- How has school education changed to cope with the modern use of computers?
- How can you see society changing further because of computer technology?

Topic 2        The Internet
- What are some of the advantages and disadvantages of modern access to the Internet?
- Do you think people spend too long on the Internet?
- What dangers are involved in using the Internet?
- How do you think life with the Internet will change over the next 20 years?

# PRACTICE TEST 8

## LISTENING

 Download audio recordings for the test here:
http://www.ielts-blog.com/ielts-practice-tests-downloads/

### SECTION 1        Questions 1 – 10

**Questions 1 – 5**

Complete the Sunshine Tours customer details form below.

Write **NO MORE THAN THREE WORDS AND/OR A NUMBER** from the listening for each answer.

<table>
<tr><td colspan="2" align="center">**Sunshine Tours**<br>**Customer Details**</td></tr>
<tr><td>*Example*</td><td>*Answer*</td></tr>
<tr><td>Type of Holiday:</td><td>*<u>Cruise</u>*</td></tr>
<tr><td>Customers' Names:</td><td>1    Keith Waters        Age: 32<br>       Melissa<br>2    **(1)** _____ Waters    Age: **(2)** ___30___<br><br>(no children)</td></tr>
<tr><td>Interests & Hobbies:</td><td>Travelling, swimming, jogging, **(3)** _Cinema_,<br>history, reading</td></tr>
<tr><td>Budget:</td><td>$7000 - $**(4)** _11000_</td></tr>
<tr><td>Dates:</td><td>1st July - 16th July</td></tr>
<tr><td>Cruise Duration:</td><td>At least **(5)** _14 nights_</td></tr>
</table>

## Questions 6 – 10

Complete Keith's notes below.

Write **NO MORE THAN TWO WORDS AND/OR A NUMBER** for each answer.

<table>
<tr><td>

<u>Maria Cristina</u>

Spanish boat

Starts in Barcelona

Cost - $10,500 (not including **(6)** _flights_

All food and drinks included

Inside cabin (upgrade to sea view for $800)

On board cinema (different films every night)

**(7)** _Lectures_ on destinations

Classes (ie. painting, cooking, art appreciation and others)

**(8)** _grand instrum._ included

</td><td>

<u>Sea Queen</u>

Spanish boat

Starts in Marseille

Length - 2½ week cruise

Cost - $**(9)** _9000_ (including flights)

Sea view cabin

Food included, but not drinks (water free)

Cinema

**(10)** _swimming pool_ + gym

</td></tr>
</table>

## SECTION 2        *Questions 11 – 20*

*Questions 11 – 15*

*Complete the sentences below.*

Use **NO MORE THAN TWO WORDS/AND OR A NUMBER** *from the listening for each answer.*

11     The Read for All charity especially targets _low income_ parents.

12     The Read for All charity mainly tries to contact parents at _hospitals_.

13     Parents who want help with finding books can go to the Read for All charity's centre or visit their _website_.

14     The Read for All charity's app costs _$1._ to download to a smartphone.

15     _Immigrant_ families can also benefit the Read for All charity in terms of improving English for the whole family.

*Questions 16 – 18*

*Choose the correct letter A, B, or C.*

16     The Read for All charity gets most of its operating funds from

     **A**     the government.
     **B**     one individual.
     **C**     the general public.

17     Jake suggests radio listeners can make a donation to the Read for All charity

     **A**     online.
     **B**     by dropping into one of the charity's centres.
     **C**     by post.

18     The Read for All charity can sometimes pay

     **A**     a modest hourly rate for people who work for them.
     **B**     for some overnight accommodation if volunteers live far from a centre.
     **C**     for workers' expenses if they provide a receipt.

**Page 52**

## Questions 19 and 20

*Below is a basic map used to show where the Read for All Charity's offices are. The map has 12 locations marked **A - L**. Match the locations in questions **19 and 20** with the correct locations on the map and write the correct letter (**A - L**) next to questions **19 and 20**.*

**19**     Cinema                              J / G

**20**     Main Town Post Office        I

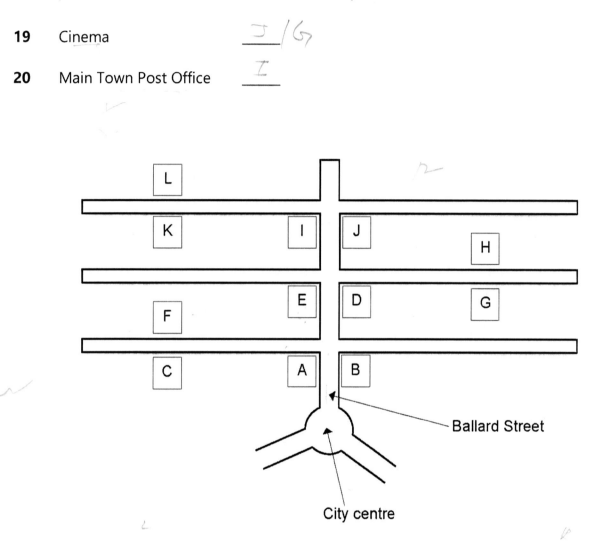

## SECTION 3          Questions 21 – 30

### Questions 21 – 25

Complete the table below on the essay status of two of Mr. Stevenson's students.

Write **NO MORE THAN TWO WORDS** from the listening for each answer.

| | Subject | Problems | Recommendations |
|---|---|---|---|
| AMY | | | |
| | World (21) _____ and the car industry | (22) _____ of her sources | Check the (23) _____ on the department website |
| WILLIAM | | | |
| | How (24) _____ affects employment in Northern Territory | Written too much | Focus on the (25) _____ of his essay - going through the essay and improving the style will cut many words |

**Questions 26 – 30**

*Choose the correct letter **A, B, or C**.*

26      Why was Anna delayed starting her essay this month?

     **A**     She was sick
     **B**     She had other work to prepare
     **C**     Her parents were visiting

27      Where does Mr. Stevenson recommend that Anna study?

     **A**     The library
     **B**     Mr. Stevenson's dedicated study periods
     **C**     Quietly at home

28      What does Mr. Stevenson ask Anna to provide him with for an extension?

     **A**     A copy of the department rules
     **B**     A paper from her doctor
     **C**     An application form for the extension

29      What was Anna's first possible topic to write about?

     **A**     Foreign investment helped by reduced tax deals offered by the Australian government
     **B**     Australian taxes invested in overseas investment
     **C**     How foreign governments' tax deals help Australian businesses invest overseas

30      What was Anna's second possible topic to write about?

     **A**     The travel business in Australia and New Zealand
     **B**     Taxation issues between Australia and New Zealand
     **C**     A history of trade between Australia and New Zealand

## SECTION 4      *Questions 31 – 40*

### Questions 31 – 35

*Match the person or people (questions 31 - 35) with their actions (A - G).*

*Write the correct letter (A - G) next to questions 31 - 35.*

**31**      The Sumerians  D

**32**      The Roman Emperor Valentinian  C

**33**      Camilo Baldi  F

**34**      Jean Michon  E

**35**      Wilheim Preyer  A

**A**      Stressed the importance of the link between handwriting and brain functions

**B**      Was the first paid for his autograph

**C**      Wrote the first signature in handwriting that we still have

**D**      Used seals to identify ownership

**E**      Started a school of graphology

**F**      First wrote about the science that was to be called graphology

**G**      Interpreted handwriting for the police

## Questions 36 – 40

*Complete the summary of the development of the e-signature.*

*Write **NO MORE THAN TWO WORDS** from the listening for each answer.*

---

**The Development of the e-signature**

E-signatures have made the hand-written signature (**36**) _____. [obsolete]
Technologies such as the fax and the Internet created a need for contracts and agreements to be signed without the presence of the signer. E-signatures did not satisfy previous basic law requirements for hand-written signatures, as they did not create a (**37**) _____. [mark / trace] The UN created a (**38**) _____ [framework's] in 1996 that set out rules that allowed electronic business to go ahead, as e-contracts and paper contracts would meet with (**39**) _____ [obstacles] in law. Although online businesses can use 'click-to-agree', there is still demand for an electronic hand-written signature, as it can help (**40**) _____ [verification] in law and create a human touch. This kind of hand-written signature is available on software used to create electronic signatures.

---

# READING

## SECTION 1        *Questions 1 – 14*

### Questions 1 – 7

*Answer the questions below.*

*Write **NO MORE THAN THREE WORDS AND/OR A NUMBER** from the text for each answer.*

*Write your answers in boxes **1 - 7** on your answer sheet.*

1        For how long has Lanscombe Farm been in the organic food business?

2        What information will potential customers need to find out the Lanscombe Farm delivery charge?

3        What do people have to provide with their email address in order to set up an account?

4        For what payment method does Lanscombe farm not charge extra?

5        How often are the Lanscombe Farm's open days?

6        What does sourcing locally help Lanscombe Farm to minimise?

7        What is the source of Lanscombe Farm's cheese?

## Lanscombe Farm

*refresh your diet today!*

We've been growing and selling organic fruit and vegetables on our farm now for twenty years and we offer a home delivery of vegetables and/or fruit to your doorstep. You can set up regular deliveries of our selections and/or you can order bespoke selections delivered when and where you want them. Deliveries are free within a certain distance of our farm. A modest delivery fee is charged after that. Customers should go to our website and put their postcode into our rangefinder to see how much it is to get our products to them.

In order to organise deliveries, you need to set up an account with us. Go to our website and click on the icon OPEN AN ACOUNT. All you need to give us is your email address and of course a password. You don't pay anything until you order something.

Although you are welcome to telephone us at any time to discuss our products and hear what's seasonal, payment is done only by card on our website. In this way, your payments are always secure. Credit cards are subject to a small fee dependent on the type of card, but debit cards are free. Details of your credit or debit cards are never held or stored by us and the actual card purchases are done through a third party, which specialises in this service and therefore offers the best of security.

For customers of our weekly delivery, boxes are sent out every Friday, so you have all your fruit and vegetables ready for the weekend. In your box, you'll have a selection of seasonal fruit and vegetables, which are guaranteed to be fresh and organic. If you need produce at short notice, we also have a farm shop, which is open from 8 a.m. to 7 p.m. from Monday to Saturday. The shop stocks all the produce that we sell for delivery, but of course you can come and pick things up whenever you want.

If you are as serious about your fresh fruit and vegetables as we are, we would expect that you might want to visit us and see where and how your food is produced. We have open days twice a year and you can wander around our fields, greenhouses and packing rooms and meet all of our team who prepare your food.

We don't grow all the fruit and vegetables that we sell, so we're very careful about how we source anything that we buy. First of all, we try and buy from producers as close to us as possible, which cuts down on our carbon footprint. After that we look further afield for anything that we can't find locally. Finally, we source some things from overseas. Air freight is rarely used, but we do often choose imported vegetables that are in season in their country of origin. All the places that supply us are visited annually, including overseas suppliers. This allows us to build up personal relationships as well as ensuring that what we receive is fresh and organic. For details about all the farms that supply us, please consult our website. We provide details on all the farms, including information on their farming methods and organic approaches.

We don't only deliver organic fruit and vegetables, but we also have regular deliveries of fresh dairy products and eggs from local organic farms. Furthermore, our nearest bakery supplies us with an amazing range of bread, rolls, cakes, pies and tarts that you should try.

*Check our website out now!!!*

## Questions 8 – 11

*Complete the summary below.*

*Write **NO MORE THAN THREE WORDS** from the text for each answer.*

*Write your answers in boxes **8 - 11** on your answer sheet*

---

### Cut your Energy Bills - Solar Power

Using solar energy can drastically cut your bills and help the environment. Enough solar panels were installed last year to power 130,000 homes, even, thanks to photovoltaic electric panels, in places where it's not sunny all the time. Those interested should consider four points: *A.* A quality solar energy system is a (**8**) _____. Choose a system with a centralized hybrid power management system and the latest batteries. *B.* A good installation company can help with opportunities in obtaining (**9**) _____ and explaining funding possibilities. Installers should have the proper (**10**) _____ and memberships. *C.* Your solar system should suit your home, needs and sun exposure. The solar panels should be placed to take advantage of the Sun and light and it should adjust itself automatically to the position of the Sun. *D.* Your solar panels should have been tested to be equal or better than the panels' nameplate power rating to ensure they are good as they should be. Check too on your potential system's (**11**) _____ in case there's a future problem. Dependent on various factors, but mainly the set-up's size, excess electricity can be sold at various rates to your energy supplier. Use of a certified installer is mandatory.

---

## Cut your Energy Bills - Solar Power

*Are you fed up with excessive electricity bills? Well, look no further than solar energy systems.*

Did you know that you could cut your electrical costs and show off your environmental savvy by installing solar panels? Last year, 792 megawatts of new residential solar systems were put online in the U.S., which is enough to power the equivalent of more than 130,000 homes.

Many people believe that their homes are not 'sunny' enough to warrant installing solar energy, but this is not the case nowadays. Modern installations use photovoltaic electric panels, which generate electricity when exposed to any light and even when it's not a sunny day!

Think you might want to give solar panels a try? Think about these four key points:

**Quality Products.** Solar panels are a long-term investment in your home; you want them to last. A quality system should last for at least 25 years. You should ensure you choose a system with the most modern technology with a centralized hybrid power management system that can switch power from Grid, Solar or both intelligently. Ensure, too, to get the latest battery technologies that offer better safety, an excellent cycle life and a higher dynamic charge acceptance. All this will provide a lower total cost of ownership and better power reliability for household and/or business.

**Experienced Installation.** A qualified, experienced installer not only designs your solar panels, but can also save you money by guiding you through the process of securing tax rebates and financing options. It's important to choose an installer who has the correct credentials and who is a member of the right professional bodies. If an installer is a certified member, it means that he will have been properly trained and inspected and his/her work will all be covered by insurance. Having a certified installer is also important if you wish to sell any excess electricity that you generate (see below).

**Intelligent Design.** Your residential solar system must be designed to produce the right amount of power for your home and lifestyle. A good installer will review your previous year's energy bills and analyse the orientation and shading of your roof to determine the best design. Solar panels must be placed so that they maximise the exposure to the light and the sun. As angles of the sun differ depending on the time of the year, it's best to have a system that will make the small adjustments to maximise exposure automatically. Fortunately, the movement of the Earth in relation to the Sun is predictable, so effective programmable systems are easy enough to find.

**Guaranteed Performance.** Be sure to choose solar panels that have gone through a factory-tested process called "plus sorting", which ensures the panels have met or exceeded their nameplate power rating. Panels that don't undergo this process are as much as 5 per cent less efficient than advertised. And don't forget the warranty - solar panels are constantly exposed to the elements and can degrade; you need to ensure your protection.

*Earn Money!* You can apply to get payments from your energy supplier if you generate your own electricity. This is called a 'feed-in tariff'. If your application is successful, you'll get a set amount for each unit of electricity you generate. The rates depend especially on the size of your system, but also on what technology you install, when your system was installed and how energy efficient your home is. You'll also need to use a certified installer for whatever solar system you use.

**Questions 12 – 14**

*Do the following statements agree with the information given in the text below?*

*In boxes 12 – 14 on your answer sheet write:*

> **TRUE**            *if the statement agrees with the information*
> **FALSE**           *if the statement contradicts the information*
> **NOT GIVEN**    *if there is no information on this*

12    Employees will be notified of any fire evacuation practices two weeks before they take place.

13    Visitors to the building must always wear a visible, plastic ID on a cord around their necks.

14    Locks must never be used on windows or doors during a fire evacuation practice.

---

**Brelford Town Hall Fire Practices**

We are required by the district fire services to perform two fire evacuation practices every year without notice to staff. We must tell the fire services two weeks in advance when these fire evacuation practices will be and they might come and observe how they are being conducted. The fire services can direct us to do more if they are not satisfied with our performance. Mandatory fire training will be held twice a year.

Employees should be aware of and follow the following instructions:

* All employees must be aware of the evacuation procedures that are posted in every room and they should be aware of all the evacuation exits that can be used in the case of an emergency.
* Visitors to the building must sign in and out when they arrive.
* All employees should let their department secretary know when they leave the building.
* All employees must gather quietly at a muster point after evacuating the building.
* Heads of department must perform a roll call of their staff and report anyone missing to the building manager.
* The building manager will check to see that all visitors are out of the building.
* All windows and doors should be shut (but not secured) when people are evacuating the building.

---

## SECTION 2        Questions 15 – 27

### Questions 15 – 21

Complete the notes below.

Write **NO MORE THAN TWO WORDS** for each answer.

Write your answers in boxes **15 - 21** on your answer sheet.

---

**APPRENTICESHIPS WITH BOWMAN'S BUILDING**

Bowman's carries out a variety of building projects and is a large employer. The government has created (**15**) _____ to help Bowman's train a steady supply of skilled craftsmen through apprenticeships that could lead to a (**16**) _____, work in other companies or the chance to go into business. Classwork in (**17**) _____, combined with workplace time will teach apprentices trade skills and give them the chance of acquiring a nationally recognised qualification.

| Apprenticeship Components | |
|---|---|
| Classroom | * Supervised by teachers<br>* A bad attendance record or bad results can mean the end of the apprenticeship |
| Workplace | * A normal working situation<br>* Apprentices gain skills and experience<br>* Apprentices can best learn through asking questions and experimenting<br>* Each apprentice is assigned to a (**18**) _____ (fully trained to instruct and assess young people)<br>* Over the apprenticeship period, apprentices will interact with different people and develop important interpersonal skills. |

Apprentices will be paid a wage (the amount is dependent on the apprenticeship) and any costs will be met. Holiday entitlement is the same as for regular workers at Bowman's. (**19**) _____ might also be available.

The apprenticeship will be challenging, but (**20**) _____. Applications for an apprenticeship are to be done on Bowman's (**21**) _____.

---

# Bowman's Building – Opportunities for Apprentices

Bowman's Building (or Bowman's as we are known) is a nationwide company that is involved in the building of housing estates, business parks and government projects. We employ hundreds of people at any one time and we also contract in various other businesses when needed. In order to sustain the supply of skilled craftsmen, the government has offered Bowman's subsidies in order to train apprentices. Successful apprentices might find a permanent job with us, they might work in similar businesses or maybe they will go out and start their own business.

Our apprenticeships are carried out in partnership with local colleges and your training will include classroom as well as building site time. If successful, you will end the apprenticeship with practical trade skills and a nationally recognised qualification.

In the classroom component, you will work under the close supervision of class teachers. You will follow the timetable provided and a poor attendance record or extremely poor grades can result in your apprenticeship being stopped.

In the workplace component, you'll be placed in a normal working situation. You'll gain skills and use the actual tools, equipment and materials that you'll be using when you're fully trained. Each apprentice will be allocated a qualified tradesperson. He/she will be responsible for making sure you acquire the skills needed to pass the practical part of your apprenticeship. If you have any questions about techniques, terminology or anything related to the industry, you can instantly ask. Asking questions, taking on more responsibility and trying new things will help you get better in your apprenticeship. All these tradespeople will have had company training on how to teach young people and how to assess you critically, helpfully and fairly.

Apprenticeships are not only about work skills. Apprenticeships typically take between one and four years to complete, depending on the type of apprenticeship and the level. In this time, you will forge relationships and contacts with clients, colleagues, and managers. You will learn how to deal with all these various types of people and acquire key interpersonal abilities.

As an apprentice, you'll be paid a weekly wage and your college fees and any registration costs will be paid by Bowman's and/or the government. The amount you are paid will depend on the type of apprenticeship that you choose. While on your apprenticeship, you'll be treated like a regular employee of Bowman's and this means that you'll get a certain amount of paid holiday per year in addition to bank holidays. Your entitlement may vary depending on your particular apprenticeship, but by law you are entitled to at least 20 days. You may also be able to take some time off for study leave in addition to your usual paid leave, but this again depends on the type of apprenticeship you have.

Your apprenticeship will be very rewarding, even if at times it may seem demanding. Once you have finished your apprenticeship, you'll have a world of options open to you. You may be able to carry on working with us or you can look for a relevant job in a different company.

In order to apply for an apprenticeship with us, you will need to visit our website (www.bowmansbuilding.com). Click on the APPRENTICESHIPS icon and follow the on-screen instructions.

**Questions 22 – 27**

*Complete the table below.*

*Write **NO MORE THAN TWO WORDS** from the text for each answer.*

*Write your answers in boxes **22 - 27** on your answer sheet.*

| Types of Dismissal | |
|---|---|
| **Fair** | * Employers mustn't dismiss people without a valid reason - there are various. <br> * Court procedure unnecessary. |
| **Unfair** | * Can be claimed for any dismissal. <br> * Example reasons: the employers lied over the cause of the dismissal, the cause was unfair and the employer's behaviour was (**22**) _____. |
| **Constructive** | * Because an employer breaks the employment contract. <br> * Example Reasons: wage cuts, demotion, harassment, overworking or dangerous conditions. <br> * This isn't automatically (**23**) _____, but hard for an employer to prove otherwise. |
| **Wrongful** | * When an employer acts improperly in the dismissal process. <br> * An employee might claim unfair dismissal at an (**24**) _____. |
| **Summary** | * When an employee is dismissed immediately without benefits, normally due to gross misconduct, which is bad enough to cancel the employee's contract. <br> * Companies' (**25**) _____ should publish examples of gross misconduct. <br> * Companies must take care with this dismissal - a tribunal may approve a (**26**) _____ for unfair dismissal. |
| **Suspension** | * Suspending an employee while receiving (**27**) _____ can keep the employee away from the office at a potentially awkward time. <br> * Suspension must never imply guilt. |

# Dismissal - Notes for UK Employers and Employees

Dismissal is when an employer ends an employee's contract. There are five types of dismissal in UK law:

<u>Fair</u>

Employers are required to have a valid reason to dismiss employees. This can be if they're incapable of doing their job to the required standard, they're capable, but unwilling to do their job properly or if they've committed some form of misconduct. There's no reason for employers to go through the courts, as long as they act fairly.

<u>Unfair Dismissal</u>

If employers dismiss an employee, the employee can still claim unfair dismissal. This could be because of a variety of reasons, including the cause the employer gave for the dismissal wasn't the real one, the reason the employer gave was unfair or the employer was unreasonable in their actions, e.g. by failing to give them plenty of warning about the dismissal.

<u>Constructive Dismissal</u>

This is when an employee resigns because an employer breached the employment contract. This could be a single serious event or a series of less serious events. An employee could claim constructive dismissal if an employer cuts their wages, demotes them, allows harassment, increases workload unfairly or makes them work in hazardous surroundings. A constructive dismissal isn't necessarily unfair, but it would be difficult for an employer to show that a breach of contract was fair.

<u>Wrongful Dismissal</u>

This is where an employer doesn't follow correct procedures during the dismissal process. If an employee thinks an employer has dismissed them unfairly, constructively or wrongfully, the employee might take the employer to an employment tribunal.

<u>Summary Dismissal</u>

This is when an employer dismisses someone instantly without notice or pay in lieu of notice, usually because of gross misconduct. Generally speaking, an act of gross misconduct is considered to be serious enough to overturn the contract between employer and employee, so justifying summary dismissal. What an organisation regards as this kind of misbehaviour should be clear from its disciplinary rules. Typically, they might include such things as theft or fraud, physical violence, gross negligence, incapacity due to alcohol or illegal drugs, and serious insubordination. A fair procedure must still be followed. Failing to establish the facts before taking action and holding a meeting with the employee, and denying the employee the right to appeal is highly likely to be considered unfair and lead to a claim against the employer.

*Suspension* For any dismissal, It may not be appropriate for the employee to be at work while facts are established, so a short period of suspension on full pay may be helpful. But a suspension should only be imposed after careful consideration. It should be made clear to the employee that it is not in itself a disciplinary action and does not involve any prejudgement.

## SECTION 3        *Questions 28 – 40*

*Read the following text and answer Questions 28 – 40.*

### Water Stress and Scarcity

Water stress and scarcity occur when there is an imbalance between the availability of water and the demand for water. When we hear people talking about water stress and scarcity, we often think of drought, but this is only one of several causes. Alex Karpov, a representative from the World Health Organisation, explains some of the other issues that also impact the availability of fresh water. "The deterioration of ground water and surface water quality, competition for water between different segments of society, for example, between agricultural, industrial, and domestic users, and even social and financial barriers, are all causes of water stress and scarcity today."

While approximately three quarters of the Earth are covered by water, only a small proportion of it is accessible as fresh water. Of the accessible fresh water supplies, nearly 70 per cent is withdrawn and used for irrigation to produce food, and the demand just keeps growing. Although there is currently no global scarcity of water, more and more regions of the world are chronically short of water. At present, 1.1 billion people have little choice but to use potentially harmful sources of water, and 2.6 billion people, which is around half the developing world, lack access to adequate sanitation. As Kathie Coles, an executive from the charity World of Water, describes, the situation will deteriorate. "Over the next 20 years, an estimated 1.8 billion people will be living in countries or regions with an absolute water scarcity, and two-thirds of the world population may be under stress conditions. This situation will only worsen, as rapidly growing urban areas place heavy pressure on water supplies."

Of course, there have been different initiatives put into place around the world to help with water stress and scarcity. While larger scale projects, such as the construction of piped water systems, remain important objectives of many development agencies, a shortage of time and finances will leave hundreds of millions of people without access to safe water in the foreseeable future. Georgina Ronaldson, a spokesperson for the World Bank, recently announced a way to deal with current difficulties. "To help developing countries, various concerned organisations have developed the Safe Water System (SWS), which is an adaptable and flexible intervention that employs scientific methods appropriate for the developing world."

The SWS has been criticised in various corners as being too amateurish, but Ronaldson continues to justify the approach. "The use of relevant technologies is important, as in many places around the world, water provision efforts suffer from a lack of technical knowledge to effectively manage or adapt a system to a community's fluctuating needs." The SWS is a community-based, integrative approach to improving health and quality of life through increased access to improved water, sanitation, and hygiene. Darren Stanford, a water quality engineer, explains the important three-step methodology. "The first is an assessment of the water delivery system from catchment to consumer. The second is implementing appropriate interventions, which can include protection of source waters, improvements to the water delivery system, introduction of Safe Water Systems, improved sanitation, and hygiene education. The third is the evaluation of the impact of the interventions on the health and quality of life of the consumers."

One example of how poor water access can affect local populations is the problem of guinea worm in remote parts of Africa. This is a preventable parasitic infection that affects poor communities that lack safe drinking water. The infection is transmitted to people who drink water containing copepods (tiny water fleas) that are infected with the larvae of the guinea worms. Once ingested, these larvae take up to one year to grow into adult worms; the female worms then emerge from the skin anywhere on the body. Will Goodman, a doctor with the World Health Organisation, says that this can affect communities in different ways. "The emergence of the adult female worm can be very painful, slow, and disabling and prevents people from working in their fields, tending their animals, going to school, and caring for their families."

Currently, many organisations are helping the last nine endemic countries (all in sub-Saharan Africa) to eradicate guinea worm. Since the Guinea Worm Eradication Program began, the incidence of guinea worm disease has declined from 3.5 million cases per year in 20 endemic countries to 25,018 reported cases in 2006 from the 9 remaining endemic countries. The eradication efforts make use of simple interventions for providing safe drinking water, including using cloth filters and pipe filters to strain the infected copepods from the water, applying chemicals to the water supplies to kill the larvae, and preventing infected people from entering and contaminating the water supplies, as the worms emerge from their skin. Providing borehole wells and other supplies of safe drinking water in endemic villages is another important component of the eradication efforts.

The provision of borehole wells is one of the principal aims of the SWS. Many existing dug wells in communities only pierce the topsoil, do not reach deep enough and are therefore readily influenced by drought or by the natural declines from summer to autumn in the water table. SWS borehole wells can pierce the bedrock and access a deeper aquifer with water that is not affected by surface drought. These are also unaffected by guinea worm infestation and the water is much safer for human consumption.

## Questions 28 – 34

*Look at the following statements (questions 28 - 34) and the list of people below.*

*Match each statement with the correct person's initials.*

*Write the correct initials in boxes 28 - 34 on your answer sheet.*

**28**    Local water demands around the world can sometimes change too much for the local infrastructure to cope with effectively.

**29**    The fast growth of towns will create more areas around the world suffering from water scarcity or water stress.

**30**    A measurement of the success of the implemented water intervention strategies is a key step in the Safe Water System.

**31**    A lack of money is one of the potential causes of water scarcity.

**32**    In the future, more than half of the world's population will live in an area suffering from water stress.

**33**    Poor water sanitation can lead indirectly to fewer workers being active in agriculture.

**34**    There is a current initiative today to use suitable technologies to deal with people affected by water difficulties around the world.

| | |
|---|---|
| **AK** | Alex Karpov |
| **KC** | Kathie Coles |
| **GR** | Georgina Ronaldson |
| **DS** | Darren Stanford |
| **WG** | Will Goodman |

**Questions 35 – 38**

*Choose the correct letter **A, B, C or D**.*

*Write the correct letter in boxes **35 - 38** on your answer sheet.*

35      Over two-thirds of the Earth's available fresh water

      **A**      is inaccessible by equatorial communities.
      **B**      is becoming heavily polluted.
      **C**      is used for farming.
      **D**      is used by industry.

36      Some of the bigger initiatives implemented by many organisations

      **A**      lack the money to help people for some time.
      **B**      are affected by corruption.
      **C**      do not get the required government backing.
      **D**      are obstructed by bureaucracy.

37      A Safe Water System project begins with

      **A**      a finance assessment of the whole scheme.
      **B**      a decision regarding whether new or improved water systems are needed.
      **C**      an evaluation of how water needs to reach people in any given community.
      **D**      a hygiene evaluation of the affected area.

38      Some of methods used to combat guinea worm contamination

      **A**      have failed, because of a lack of funding.
      **B**      are easy to implement.
      **C**      have made the situation worse.
      **D**      require trainers to visit the communities.

## Questions 39 and 40

Label the diagram below.

Write **NO MORE THAN TWO WORDS** from the text for each answer.

Write your answers in boxes **39 and 40** on your answer sheet.

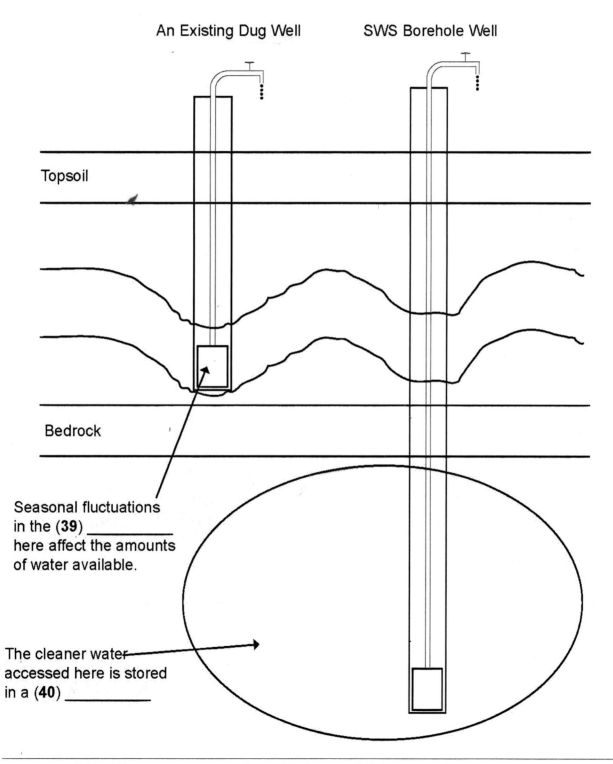

An Existing Dug Well        SWS Borehole Well

Topsoil

Bedrock

Seasonal fluctuations in the **(39)** _____ here affect the amounts of water available.

The cleaner water accessed here is stored in a **(40)** _____

# WRITING

## WRITING TASK 1

*You should spend about 20 minutes on this task.*

**You recently bought some food at a supermarket, but, when you got home, you found that the food was in bad condition.**

**Write a letter to the manager of the supermarket. In your letter,**

- **explain what happened to you**
- **give details of the day and time of the purchase**
- **ask the manager what he / she intends to do about your experience**

*You should write at least 150 words.*

*You do **NOT** need to write any addresses. Begin your letter as follows:*

***Dear Sir / Madam,***

## WRITING TASK 2

*You should spend about 40 minutes on this task.*

*Write about the following topic:*

**It seems clear that obesity in today's society is to some extent due to the availability of fast food.**

**Should governments place a tax on fast food to reduce the amount of fast food consumed?**

*Give reasons for your answer and include any relevant examples from your knowledge or experience.*

*You should write at least 250 words.*

# SPEAKING

## SECTION 1

* Can you describe to me a hotel where you have once stayed?
* Do you like staying in hotels? (Why/Why not?)
* Do you think hotels are over-priced? (Why/Why not?)

Topic 1          The Police
* What are people's attitudes to the police in your country?
* What are the qualities of a good policeman or policewoman?
* What do you think about the kind of job the police have to do?
* Do you feel the police is a suitable job for a woman? (Why/Why not?)

Topic 2          Photography
* Do you take photographs? (Why/Why not?)
* Is it important to keep photographs?
* What dangers are there nowadays with photographs and the Internet?
* Can taking a photograph of someone famous be an invasion of privacy? (Why/Why not?)

## SECTION 2

Describe a business that you know well
You should say:
          what kind of business it is
          what relationship you have with this business
          how successful this business is
and explain whether you think this is a good or bad business and why.

## SECTION 3

Topic 1          Business
* Would you like to own your own business? (Why/Why not?)
* What are the advantages and disadvantages of owning one's own business?
* What sort of things can affect the success of a business?
* How has the business environment changed over the last 30 years?

Topic 2          Charity and Helping Others
* Do you believe in giving money to organisations that help others? (Why/Why not?)
* Why do you feel organisations for helping others are necessary in today's world?
* What kind of people need the help of these organisations that help others?
* Do you think that the need for organisations for helping others will be more or less necessary in the future?

# PRACTICE TEST 9

# LISTENING

 Download audio recordings for the test here:
http://www.ielts-blog.com/ielts-practice-tests-downloads/

## SECTION 1          *Questions 1 – 10*

*Questions 1 – 5*

*Complete Sarah's People Central form below.*

*Write* **NO MORE THAN THREE WORDS AND/OR A NUMBER** *from the listening for each answer.*

| **People Central**<br>**New Potential Staff** | |
| --- | --- |
| *Example* | *Answer* |
| Type of Job Desired: | *Accountancy* |

| | |
| --- | --- |
| Name: | Mark (**1**) _____ |
| Address: | 13 Wellington Street<br>South Brisbane<br>Queensland |
| Postcode: | 4101 |
| Date of Birth: | (**2**) _____ May 1988 |
| Email Address: | markc@(**3**) _____now.com |
| Telephone:   Home:<br>                   Cell: | 07 3554 7671<br>046 9153 (**4**) _____ |
| Preferred Work Area: | The Brisbane area<br>Within a drive of approx. (**5**) _____ from home |

**Questions 6 – 10**

*Complete the sentences below.*

*Use **NO MORE THAN TWO WORDS** from the listening for each answer.*

**6**      Mark will send _____ of his professional certificates to Sarah.

**7**      Mark could happily travel to Gold Coast Printing by _____ as well as by car.

**8**      The _____ nature of the job at the import export company is a problem for Mark.

**9**      Mark is worried about _____ at a smaller company like the fishing company, Barracuda.

**10**    Mark will not need to pay a _____ for any job placement.

## SECTION 2        *Questions 11 – 20*

### Questions 11 – 17

*Complete the notes below on the Sway Road Health Centre.*

*Write* **NO MORE THAN THREE WORDS AND/OR A NUMBER** *from the listening for each answer.*

---

**Sway Road Health Centre**

Six full-time doctors
Just over (**11**) _____ patients
2 centres - Sway Road and Church Road

Registering - come during opening hours; bring a (**12**) _____, proof of address (dated within 3 months of application) and medical card (or fill out a registration from). Staff will ask for your medical history and organise a (**13**) _____ to be taken.

Appointments - contact only by phone and not by (**14**) _____. Call only during opening hours.

Opening Hours

   (**15**) _____ a.m. - 1 p.m. and 2 p.m. - 7 p.m. Monday to Friday
   (call only between 1 p.m. & 2 p.m. in an emergency)
   (closed weekends and (**16**) _____)

*The best option for emergencies is to go to hospital or call an ambulance.*

Medical Students - consultations with doctors or nurses may have a student present; there is no obligation to have a student present.

Travel Service - lots of vaccinations available. Complete a (**17**) _____ at reception - available from reception or the website. The nurse will make vaccination recommendations. Get a vaccination card. Vaccinations to be paid for on the day of vaccination.

---

### Questions 18 – 20

*Answer the questions below. Use* **NO MORE THAN THREE WORDS** *from the listening for each answer.*

**18**    Where is the suggestion box found at the health centre?

**19**    Who will deal with any complaints made?

**20**    What area is closed off during the open morning?

## SECTION 3          *Questions 21 – 30*

### Questions 21 – 25

*Match Kevin's level of satisfaction (**A - C**) with the things related to his training days (questions **21 - 25**).*

**21**     The hotel accommodation

**22**     Directions to the training

**23**     The trainer

**24**     Conference centre facilities

**25**     The other trainees

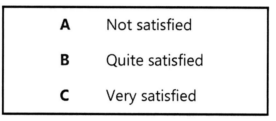

|   |   |
|---|---|
| **A** | Not satisfied |
| **B** | Quite satisfied |
| **C** | Very satisfied |

### Questions 26 – 30

*Match Kevin's problems over the weekend (**A - J**) with the solutions to the problems (questions **26 - 30**).*

**26**     Kevin had to spend some of his off-work time at the office.

**27**     The office systems were out of date.

**28**     The office systems initially wouldn't accept the new software.

**29**     A bug got into the company's computer systems.

**30**     The burglar alarm went off in the offices.

| A | Kevin bought replacement computers | F | Kevin received some extra holiday time |
|---|---|---|---|
| B | More antivirus protection was needed | G | Kevin hired a consultant |
| C | Fixed by the company's antivirus protection | H | Kevin ran an update |
| D | Kevin gave a password to the security firm | I | Kevin called a friend from the training |
| E | Kevin's boss sorted the problem out | J | Kevin was paid a good bonus |

# SECTION 4       *Questions 31 – 40*

## *Questions 31 and 32*

*Complete the diagram below on the rain shadow over the Atacama Desert.*

*Write **NO MORE THAN ONE WORD** from the listening for each answer.*

*The Atacama Desert and its Rain Shadow*

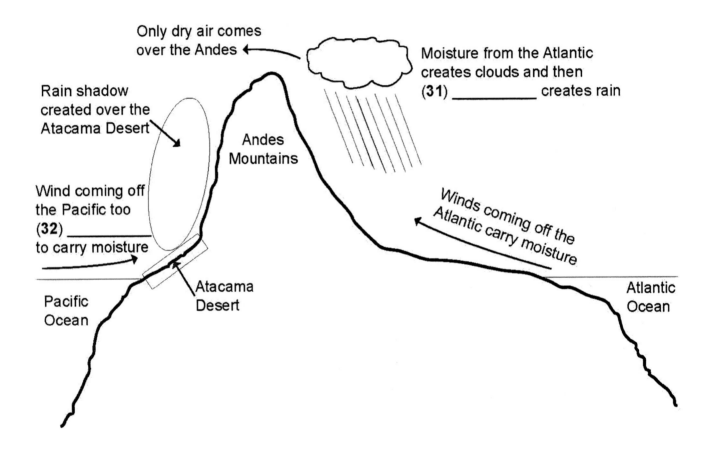

## Questions 33 – 40

Complete the notes below on the rest of the lecture on the Atacama Desert.

Write **NO MORE THAN TWO WORDS** from the listening for each answer.

---

### The Atacama Desert

The Atacama Large Millimetre Array

Because the Atacama Desert is so high and the sky overhead so clear, the Atacama Large Millimetre Array (ALMA) has been placed there. Made up of 66 antennas, its high resolution images will allow study of the earliest galaxies and the (**33**) _____ of our galaxy's planets. The ALMA is 100 times more powerful than previous similar telescopes.

The Atacama Desert

Northern ⅓ of Chile - 1000 km up to the border of Peru.
Barrier of (**34**) _____ in the west and the Andes in the east.
Average elevation is 4000m (the highest desert in the world).
Temperatures average between 0 and -25°C.

Flora and Fauna

Some life exists - local populations use some plants for (**35**) _____.
Animal life is rare, but there are some reptiles, mice and foxes.

Natural Resources and Agriculture

The Atacama was Chile's main source of income pre-World War 1.
Chile possessed a (**36**) _____ on the nitrate trade. Mines abandoned after synthetic nitrate was invented in Germany.
Other minerals are mined in the Atacama - 30% of world's (**37**) _____ is mined in the Atacama and sulphur is also extracted; these resources caused conflict with Bolivia.
Very little agriculture because of the lack of water. Some lemons, potatoes and alfalfa.

Tourism

Now a major income source.
Volcanoes, geysers, lagoons etc. attract holiday-makers and (**38**) _____.
Visitors need education to understand the (**39**) _____ of the environment.
Urbanisation and mining have caused problems.
Some farming of natural plants of the Atacama is done, interrupting their (**40**) _____.

---

Page 79

# READING

## SECTION 1        Questions 1 – 14

### Questions 1 – 7

Complete the table below.

Write **NO MORE THAN TWO WORDS** from the text for each answer.

Write your answers in boxes **1 - 7** on your answer sheet.

| The Beaver Valley Hotel - Activities for Residents | |
|---|---|
| **ACTIVITY** | **NOTES** |
| Horse Riding | * 10 minutes away<br>* (1) _____ available for adults and children<br>* Tours available with experienced (2) _____<br>* Different treks available<br>* Not too expensive<br>* Bookings at reception<br>* Book early in high season |
| Kayaking | * Hotel-owned kayaks for 1 or more people<br>* Map, (3) _____ and advice supplied by hotel<br>* 3 possible length kayak trips available<br>* Set down and pick up supplied<br>* Free for residents<br>* Bookings at reception<br>* Fishing also available<br>* Lessons and equipment available<br>* The hotel will cook any trout caught |
| Hiking | * Variety of difficulty<br>* Maps and advice provided on stops for (4) _____<br>* Range from short to whole day |
| The Local Volcano | * 7 miles away<br>* Cone-shaped hill is extinct volcano<br>* Moderate climb with (5) _____ for rests<br>* (6) _____ explain about the volcano's creation and history details<br>* Great view - even the distant mountains can be spotted sometimes<br>* Return travel by bus is very easy |
| Flea Market | * 7 a.m. start<br>* Pick up a bargain<br>* Plenty of cafés and restaurants |
| Check the (7) _____ | before you go on any outings! |

## The Beaver Valley Hotel - Activities for Residents

In our location in the Beaver Valley, we are lucky to have so many possibilities for things to do. Here is a taster of some of our favourites.

For those of you interested in horse riding, we are in partnership with a local riding club. Just 10 minutes drive away from the hotel, John will give you a wonderful time with his fantastic team of horses. They offer various things. You can get lessons for yourself and/or your child, or you can take a guided trek into the local forests and hills. You'll be taken for up to four hours around the local area to see the wonderful countryside and hopefully lots of the local animals. There are various sights to take in, such as castles, and John's guides know the area well and exactly where to go. If you enjoy it, the riding centre has various routes to offer, so, if you're not too stiff, you can do a different trek later in the week. They're very reasonably priced, so ask us at reception to give John a call to make a booking. Do bear in mind though that they can get very busy at high season, so if you're interested, get in touch with us as early as you can (even before you arrive at the hotel) and we'll make sure you get a booking.

As we are next to the Beaver River, we decided to buy a range of one-person and two-people kayaks. We'll take you to a good starting point on the river and give you a map, so you know where you're going. For safety, there are life vests provided and we'll give you some hints on kayaking. Then, after two, four or six hours, we'll pick you up at pre-arranged points. The river never flows that fast and is not deep, so this is a safe outing for all the family. This activity is free of charge for residents of the hotel, so come to reception again to make a booking. As well as being home to Beavers, the Beaver River is also stocked with a lot of wild brown trout. The Hotel owns the fishing rights to both banks on a stretch near the hotel and fishing is free for residents. We can rent you all the equipment for a nominal fee and there's a local expert available who can give fishing lessons and tell you where to fish. Limited numbers of trout over a certain size may be taken from the river and the hotel chef will be delighted to cook them just the way you like them.

If horses and water are not your thing, there are lots of hiking trails, which range from easy to demanding. We have plenty of maps of the trails and advice on places to pause for refreshments. Hikes vary from a one-hour stroll to all-day walks that will tire you out and sharpen your appetite for dinner.

About seven miles from the hotel, you may have seen a modestly-sized conical hill. It's a local secret that this hill is actually an extinct volcano from millions of years ago. It's been eroding all that time, so it's not that difficult a climb and there are well-tended paths with benches on which to take a break. In addition, there are lots of information boards scattered around, so that you can learn about the formation of the volcano and its history. When you reach the top, there is a magnificent view and, on a clear day, you can even see the distant mountain range. Buses leave from outside the hotel every hour, on the hour, and return with the same frequency.

Every Sunday, the local market town holds a flea market. It begins at 7 a.m., so get up and get there early to see if you can pick up a bargain. The market square also has lots of cafés and restaurants, so if you've done enough browsing, you can make yourself comfortable and sip a tea, coffee or cold drink.

*As you can see, lots of our activities are outside, so make sure you inform yourself regarding the weather forecast to avoid getting too wet (if that bothers you!).*

**Questions 8 – 14**

The text on the following page has 7 sections (**A – G**).

Choose the correct heading for each section from the list of headings below.

Write the correct number (**i – x**) in boxes **8 – 14** on your answer sheet.

| | |
|---|---|
| i | Exchanging your Old Printer |
| ii | Running out of Ink |
| iii | Starting to Print |
| iv | Troubleshooting |
| v | Safety Instructions |
| vi | Printing Materials |
| vii | Positioning your New Printer |
| viii | How to Clear Blockages |
| ix | Printer Maintenance |
| x | Using Coloured Inks |

8    Section A    v

9    Section B    vii

10   Section C    iii

11   Section D    ix

12   Section E    ii

13   Section F    x

14   Section G    iv

## Using your New Electronix Printer

**A**      Your new Electronix printer is an electronic device and you should therefore always observe some basic precautions: connect your printer to properly grounded electricity outlets, replace any damaged or frayed cables, don't open or try and fix your printer yourself, and unplug your printer whilst replacing the ink cartridge. If you are leaving the place where your printer is for over a week, it's a sensible precaution to unplug your printer while you are away. Try not to have drinks near the printer, as any liquids spilled onto it can have catastrophic effects to the electronic components. Spilled liquids can cause short circuits and even lead to fires!

**B**      Do not block or cover the openings in the printer's cabinet. Keep your new Electronix printer away from excessive direct sunlight and put it on a secure table that will not fall over easily. Put your printer in a place away from children - children are fascinated by printers and love sticking their fingers in them.

**C**      When you connect your new Electronix printer to your computer, you should be able to print straight away, as most computers have all common printer software already installed. If you cannot print, you will be able to find the driver software online or on the CD that is provided with your new Electronix printer. Before printing anything important on your new Electronix printer, it's a good idea to print a few test pages in order to check that everything is working correctly.

**D**      Your new Electronix printer will work with all sizes of standard printer paper. Do not use any metallised paper in it, as this will not work. Do not try and print using any plastic sheets or plastic coated paper. Your new Electronix printer uses heat in its printing process, which will melt any plastic used. Any damage to an Electronix printer caused by using plastic coated paper will invalidate the warranty.

**E**      Your ink cartridge can be replaced at most reputable high street dealers or you can order one online on our website. Consult your instruction manual or our website for instructions on how to replace your cartridge. It can be tempting to use a cheap ink-refill service, but using a different brand of ink in your new Electronix printer will invalidate your warranty.

**F**      Your new Electronix printer does not require any servicing, but cleaning it periodically can extend its life and performance - a good time for doing this can be when you're changing your ink cartridge. Use only damp soft tissues or a soft brush for cleaning and don't use any chemicals. When cleaning your printer, always unplug it first and allow it to cool if it has recently been switched on. It's also best to remove any paper from the paper tray to avoid any drips.

**G**      If your printer malfunctions in any way, check our *Problems with your Printer* guide that is available on our website. Follow the instructions given there. We have found that 80% of customer problems are resolved using our guide. If there are still problems after using our guide, go to one of the recommended repair outlets that are also available on our website. If your printer is still under warranty, all repair or parts costs or any full printer replacement costs will not have to be paid for.

## SECTION 2        Questions 15 – 27

### Questions 15 – 21

*Complete the flow chart below.*

*Write **NO MORE THAN THREE WORDS** from the text for each answer.*

*Write your answers in boxes **15 – 21** on your answer sheet.*

### Our Employee Appraisal Process

---

**1. The Interview**       The job description used at the employee's original interview will outline the roles and responsibilities; these will be formalised in the employee's **(15)** _contract_

↓

**2. 3-month Review**   This ends the employee's **(16)** _probation period_ and ensures things are going smoothly.

↓

**3. Before the Annual Meeting**        **(17)** _notice_ of the annual meeting should be given 2 weeks before, so that the employee can prepare and submit a **(18)** _self-evaluation statement_ covering five key points.

↓

**4. The Meeting**       Appropriate time should be set aside and it should be fairly **(19)** _informal_ to create an effective atmosphere. The meeting will discuss what the employee submitted before the meeting.

↓

**5. The (20)** _rating_ **(part of the meeting)**   Although the employee gives input, the manager alone awards this.

↓

**6. The Report**         This will be written by the manager and sent to the employee within a week of the meeting.

↓

**7. The Second Meeting**       The report is discussed and signed by manager and employee.

↓

**8. Appeal**     If desired, employees can use the appeal process laid out in the company handbook, found by clicking the correct **(21)** _tab_ on the Intranet, at reception or with a line manager.

---

## Our Employee Appraisal Process

Employees in our organisation are clearly engaged in their work and doing their best for our organisation. In order to recognise employees' commitment, we run an annual appraisal program. In a way, the program begins with when an employee is interviewed for his/her job. The job description will have outlined the roles and responsibilities of the employee's position. The contract will then stipulate these things officially. Copies of all relevant employment documentation should be kept by the employee, the human resources department and the line manager of the employee concerned.

The appraisal process of an employee should begin a year after the employment began with the first annual review, although there will be a 3-month review of the employee at the conclusion of the probation period. The three-month review allows both employer and employee to be sure that their commitment to each other is warranted. Both employer and the employee have the right to end the employment with a week's notice at any point up to or including the 3-month review.

Before the annual meeting, the employee should receive at least two weeks' notice. If the employee is unable to be present at the meeting date and time offered, he/she should contact his/her line manager as soon as possible in order to arrange a suitable date for the meeting to take place. The employee should give a self-evaluation statement to the manager(s) conducting the meeting giving his/her views of his/her performance over the year in terms of the roles and responsibilities. The employee can ask his/her line manager for help with this if they so wish. He/she should note:

* what things are perceived to have gone well over the year
* what things should have gone better over the year
* how things should be improved over the next year
* potential targets in the coming year for the company and the employee's personal growth
* the salary for the employee over the coming year

There should be plenty of time allocated to the appraisal meeting. It should be reasonably informal, so that the employee is at ease and can discuss his/her performance without any undue pressure. The agenda of the meeting will follow the five points referred to above, although other relevant points can be raised.

At the end of the meeting, there will be a rating of the employee's performance. The employee will give his/her input regarding this, however, awarding it will be the sole responsibility of the manager(s) conducting the appraisal. The employee will be outstanding, standard or unsatisfactory. This should not be communicated to the employee at the appraisal.

After the meeting, the manager will write up a report and present it to the employee within a week. The rating will be included within this report. There will then be a second meeting with the employee to discuss this report to ensure that it is fair and then both the manager and the employee should sign it when they are happy with it. The report will form a basis for the following year's annual appraisal meeting. If there is any conflict over the report, then there is an appeal process for the employee. Employees should consult the company handbook to inform themselves about this process. This can be located under the appropriate tab on the company Intranet or in a hard copy format at reception or with any of the line managers.

**Questions 22 – 27**

*Complete the sentences below.*

*Write **NO MORE THAN THREE WORDS** from the text for each answer.*

*Write your answers in boxes **22 - 27** on your answer sheet.*

22    An excessively formal social media policy at work could be an _____ step.

23    The _____ nature of social media developments means that social media policies can easily become out of date.

24    It can be _____ to check the social media pages of potential employees.

25    Anyone in the workplace should often check their social media _____ to stop unwanted access to their private life.

26    Companies ought to consider the _____ of their employees when dealing with the sensitive issue of social media in the workplace.

27    _____ can be missed if a social media policy is too strict.

## Using Social Media in Companies – *a guide for companies, workers and unions*

The impact of social media on the workplace is increasing. Social media is the broad term for internet-based tools used on PCs, laptops, tablets and smart phones to help people make contact, keep in touch and interact. This trend can affect communications among managers, employees and job applicants, how organisations promote and control their reputation, and how colleagues treat one another. It can also distort what boundaries there are between home and employment.

### Key Points

**Develop a policy**: Employers should include what is and what is not acceptable for general behaviour in the use at work of the Internet, emails, smart phones and social media, such as networking websites, blogs and tweets. However, it might prove impractical to have an overly formal policy that also includes rigidly covering the use of social media in recruitment.

**Rules for recruitment**: While a rigid policy on using social media in recruitment could soon become obsolete, because the trend is so dynamic, it is still advisable for an employer to have at least some rules, or procedures, which managers and employees should follow.

**Have a person responsible**: This person can be responsible for making social media usage rules. If you are a company who exploits social media for their marketing and communications, this person can coordinate the usage. This person would have to decide which media networks to use, who would manage which media accounts, what people can and can't say and what tools would be used. Professional development on this will also need to be coordinated for staff.

**Screening job candidates**: In particular when recruiting, employers should be careful if they assess applicants by looking at their social networking pages, as this could be seen as discriminatory.

**Who can see profiles?** Employees should regularly review the privacy settings on their social networking pages, as they can change. Also, they should consider whether they want or need co-workers to see those profiles.

**Talk to staff**: Employers should inform and consult their employees if planning to monitor social media activity affecting the workplace.

**Update other policies**: For example, an organisation's policy on bullying should include references to 'cyber bullying'.

**Be sensitive**: Employers should promote a work-life balance - the line between work and home is becoming increasingly blurred by the use of modern technology.

**Be flexible**: As we've mentioned above, the social media environment can change very rapidly. If you try to be too specific, you may find the policy needs updating every few months just to stay relevant. For instance, although you might list common social networks in the policy as examples, keep in mind that that the networks your business relies on may change in time. It's also important you don't impede your staff from exploring new opportunities in social media.

## SECTION 3     *Questions 28 – 40*

*Read the following passage and answer Questions 28 – 40.*

The horse used to be an indispensable part of human life and it was used for transport, war, industry, and for fun. In order to support society's dependence on the horse, whole industries grew up around it. There were sectors to breed them, shoe them, saddle them, teach people to ride them, feed them, care for them, and finally to dispose of them at the end of their useful lives. The industrial revolution and in particular the invention of the internal combustion engine was the end of the horse's central role in people's lives. Today, it seems there is a further threat to the horse that is causing a drop in its numbers. The American Horse Council (AHC) recently addressed this decline at its National Issues Forum. Leaders from various stakeholders spoke about the decrease in registered horses and the impact on their segment of the horse industry.

There has been an enthusiastic response to the forum's discussions. "People have been talking about the decline in horse numbers for some time, however, this is the first time the issue has been discussed in a comprehensive fashion," said AHC president Jay Hickey. "It was a very good program and attendees now have a better comprehension of current conditions and what actions are being taken."

Tim Capps, Director of the Equine Industry Program at the University of Louisville, gave the opening address at the forum and tried to pinpoint the reasons for the drop in today's numbers of registered horses. The economy was cited by Capps as the single largest factor, but there are probably several other factors as well. Capps believes the horse industry was in a bubble that peaked about six years before, which was similar to an earlier bubble in the 1980's. The bubble burst and caused the resulting damage to the horse industry. Capps also cited the roles of the increasing cost of horse ownership and participation in shows, concerns about welfare, and increased competition for leisure and gambling dollars.

In addition, Capps explained that there has been a decline in the number of young horses and registered horses over the last several years that is impacting all breeds and segments of the industry and the leaders of the industry are aware of this decline and are taking action. Capps also noted that this is not the first such decline in the number of horses, and in previous instances there was later a strong rebound in numbers. Examples of this were most notably during the Great Depression and in the mid-1980s. Capps pointed out the horse industry often parallels the wider economy and the current situation closely mirrors the impact the Great Depression had on the industry. In the past, the growth following such declines was often propelled by individuals outside the industry becoming interested and investing in the industry, noted Capps. He believes it will again be important to look beyond current horse industry participants to promote growth in the industry now and in the future.

Jim Gagliano, Jockey Club President, reported on the effects of the drop in numbers on the horse racing industry. "The thoroughbred foal crop has been declining and is responsible for a drop in the number of starts, number of horses in the field, the number of owners, and the number of racing days. This in turn has led to a drop in turnover for all sectors in the industry and makes the industry a less attractive one for fresh entrants and existing businesses." Forum attendees also heard what actions are being taken by the racing industry. Mr. Gagliano said that institutions are working to promote the best races and make better use of social media and online resources to attract a younger demographic, and develop new owners.

Following up on the need for more and better marketing, Patti Colbert of PCE Enterprises has come up with the Time to Ride initiative. This ambitious national campaign and contest targets the goal of giving 100,000 new people a horse experience in the following calendar year. Ms. Colbert reported that Time to Ride had accomplished its initial goal to sign up 1,000 stables, instructors, new participants and others in the horse community to host events. Colbert enthusiastically explained the next step. "These hosts will now compete for $100,000 in cash and prizes and several have already hosted their first event."

The forum also heard from associated service providers who are also being impacted. Jeff Blea, President of the American Association of Equine Practitioners (AAEP) talked about the impact on the veterinarian community and how fewer horses mean less work for horse vets. Blea additionally spoke about the AAEP programs to help veterinarians create long-term and successful relationships with horse owners and support an increase in horse breeding.

The forum has clearly identified that the problem is not only a decline in the number of registered horses, but also a decline in horse owners and people participating in horse activities. However, there is also good news, as industry organisations are taking action both individually and collectively. Hickey explains why stakeholders are not overly worried just yet. "The horse business also has one great advantage: the enduring appeal of the horse. With continued effort on the part of the entire horse community, the industry will come out of the current economic climate even more robust."

## Questions 28 – 35

Look at the following statements (questions **28 - 35**) and the list of people below.

Match each statement with the correct person's initials.

Write the correct initials in boxes **28 - 35** on your answer sheet.

**28**     The poor economic conditions in the horse industry are discouraging the starting of new horse-related businesses.

**29**     The strength of the horse business often reflects the prevalent financial climate.

**30**     Participants at the American Horse Council National Issues Forum now have an improved understanding of the issues challenging today's horse industries.

**31**     Recent promotion has already led to more people being introduced to horse riding.

**32**     Organisations related to the horse industry are improving their use of modern digital marketing.

**33**     Today's horse businesses will emerge from the slump even stronger than they were before.

**34**     Vets are also involved in helping in movements to grow the numbers of horses being born.

**35**     The lasting fascination that people have with the horse will be one reason that the industry will recover.

| | |
|---|---|
| **JH** | Jay Hickey |
| **TC** | Tim Capps |
| **JG** | Jim Gagliano |
| **JB** | Jeff Blea |
| **PC** | Patti Colbert |

## Questions 36 – 39

Do the following statements agree with the information given in the text below?

In boxes **36 – 39** on your answer sheet write:

| | |
|---|---|
| **TRUE** | if the statement agrees with the information |
| **FALSE** | if the statement contradicts the information |
| **NOT GIVEN** | if there is no information on this |

**36** The industrial revolution created an increase in the numbers of horses required in industry and transportation. *False*

**37** The horse industry has reacted well to previous drops in the number of horses. *NG*

**38** The current decline in horse numbers is still a reaction to the economic slump in the 1980's. *T*

**39** The *Time to Ride* movement has gained political as well as industry support. *NG*

## Question 40

Choose the correct letter, **A, B, C or D**.

Write the correct letter in box **40** on your answer sheet.

**40** What is the writer's purpose in the text in section 3?

**A** To explain why the American Horse Council is the best organisation to deal with the expansion of the horse industry.

**B** To review initiatives addressing current challenges to the horse industry.

**C** To describe the historical decline of the horse.

**D** To summarise organisations devoted to the welfare of the horse today.

# WRITING

## WRITING TASK 1

*You should spend about 20 minutes on this task.*

**A friend of yours has always admired your car. You have now decided to sell it.**

**Write a letter to your friend to ask if he is interested in buying your car.
In your letter,**

- **explain why you are selling your car**
- **describe the good points and any bad points about your car**
- **suggest the friend visits you to see and drive your car**

*You should write at least 150 words.*

*You do **NOT** need to write any addresses. Begin your letter as follows:*

**Dear Tim,**

## WRITING TASK 2

*You should spend about 40 minutes on this task.*

*Write about the following topic:*

**Many parents give jobs to their children to do around the house in order to develop their characters and self-sufficiency.**

**Discuss this idea and give your opinion.**

*Give reasons for your answer and include any relevant examples from your knowledge or experience.*

*You should write at least 250 words.*

# SPEAKING

## SECTION 1

- Can you describe the countryside near to where you live?
- Do you like spending time in the countryside? (Why/Why not?)
- What area of the countryside in your country would you tell a tourist to visit? (Why?)

Topic 1          Walking
- Do you like walking? (Why/Why not?)
- Why do you think people walk less today than before?
- Do you agree that walking is sometimes considered the best exercise? (Why/Why not?)
- How can we encourage people to walk more?

Topic 2          Gardens and Gardening
- Do you like gardens? (Why/Why not?)
- Is gardening popular in your country? (Why/Why not?)
- Do you think it's important for towns to have public gardens? (Why/Why not?)
- Do people in your country grow fruits and vegetables in gardens? (Why/Why not?)

## SECTION 2

Describe a memorable book that you once read
You should say:
        what this book was
        when you read it
        what happened in the book
and explain why this book is so memorable for you.

## SECTION 3

Topic 1          Reading
- Do you like reading? (Why/Why not?)
- How have attitudes to reading changed in your country over the last 50 years?
- How do you feel about how electronic books are taking over from the traditional form?
- How can we get young people to read more today?

Topic 2          Journalism
- How is the job of journalist viewed in your country?
- Do you feel censorship of journalism is a necessary thing nowadays? (Why/Why not?)
- How is news usually reported in your country?
- How do you think the reporting of news will change over the next 50 years?

# PRACTICE TEST 10

## LISTENING

 Download audio recordings for the test here:
http://www.ielts-blog.com/ielts-practice-tests-downloads/

### SECTION 1      *Questions 1 – 10*

*Questions 1 – 5*

Answer the questions below.

Use **NO MORE THAN THREE WORDS AND/OR A NUMBER** from the listening for each answer.

| Example | Answer |
|---|---|
| Which is Charlotte's preferred postcode? | *AE5* |

1      How many bedrooms does Charlotte want?

2      How much per week is Charlotte planning to spend on rent?

3      Which room does Charlotte want partially furnished?

4      What would Charlotte be responsible for if she rented an apartment with a garden?

5      What commission does Anglian Estates charge for arranging an apartment rental?

## Questions 6 – 10

Complete Charlotte's notes on the three apartments that Matthew describes.

Write **NO MORE THAN TWO WORDS** from the listening for each answer.

---

**Grantham Gardens**

First floor
Recently (**6**) _____
Right number of rooms
No garden, but a balcony with a good view
10-minute walk from St. Mary's
OK for budget
Quite a high (**7**) _____

---

**Lawrence Close**

Ground floor flat - access to garden from the (**8**) _____
150 square metre garden
Right number of rooms
Not walking distance to St. Mary's, but there is a (**9**) _____
Slightly over budget

---

**Greene Road**

Good for budget
Right number of rooms
Walking distance to St. Mary's
3rd floor (purpose-built building)
Elevator
Shared garden
(**10**) _____ kitchen and living room
Very modern
Very well looked after

---

Page 95

## SECTION 2     *Questions 11 - 20*

### Questions 11 and 12

*Below is a plan of the town square. There are **12** buildings marked **A - K**.*
*Questions **11 and 12** give **2** locations. Match the 2 locations with the correct buildings.*
*Write the correct letter (**A - K**) next to questions **11 and 12**.*

*The Town Square*

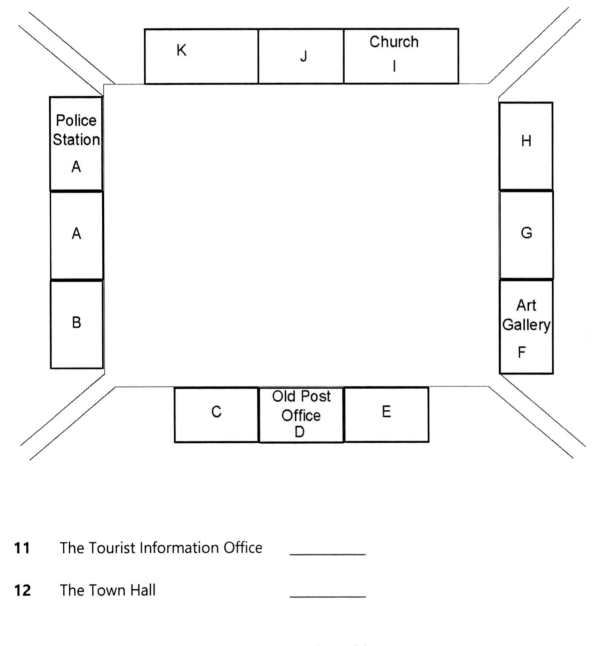

**11**     The Tourist Information Office     _____

**12**     The Town Hall     _____

## Questions 13 – 15

Choose **THREE** letters, **A - K**.

Which **THREE** of the following can happen at the new citizens' advice office?

**A**      They can find people a job

**B**      They can tell people about their holiday rights at their jobs

**C**      They can give people advice on debt

**D**      They can give people loans

**E**      They can tell people how to pay a tax bill

**F**      They can give details to people of a good accountant to use

## Questions 16 – 20

Match the situations in questions **16 - 20** with the appropriate room (**A - I**).

**16**      You're new to the area and you want to find a school for your children.

**17**      You want to give money to the citizens' advice office to help them.

**18**      You've been sacked from your job and you think it's unfair.

**19**      You want to apply for unemployment money and you don't know if you're eligible.

**20**      You've bought a second hand car from a showroom, but it's not working properly and the showroom won't help you.

| | | | |
|---|---|---|---|
| **A** | Reception | **F** | Room 18 |
| **B** | Room 1 | **G** | Room 25 |
| **C** | Room 2 | **H** | Room 27 |
| **D** | Room 4 | **I** | Room 29 |
| **E** | Room 9 | | |

Page 97

## SECTION 3      *Questions 21 – 30*

### *Questions 21 – 25*

*Match the invention (questions **21 - 25**) with the business, industry or process it affected (**A - G**).*

*Choose **FIVE** answers from the list below and write the correct letter (**A - G**) next to questions **21 - 25**.*

| 21 | The Aerosol Spray |
|----|-------------------|
| 22 | The Spinning Machine |
| 23 | The Battery |
| 24 | The Sextant |
| 25 | Light Polarisers |

| A | The mobile phone business |
|---|---------------------------|
| B | The paint business |
| C | The sunglasses business |
| D | The ship building industry |
| E | The photography business |
| F | The clothing industry |
| G | Navigation |

## Questions 26 – 28

*Choose the correct letter **A, B, or C**.*

**26**    What was the problem with using quick dry ink in fountain pens?

     A        The ink did not flow in the pen properly
     B        The ink was too soft
     C        The ink was too acidic

**27**    Who first produced a pen with a metal ball bearing at the end of a pen?

     A        Lazlo Biro
     B        John Loud
     C        An unknown earlier inventor

**28**    In which country did Biro first manufacture his ball point pens?

     A        The UK
     B        Argentina
     C        The US

## Questions 29 and 30

*Complete the diagram below on Biro's ballpoint pen.*

*Write **NO MORE THAN THREE WORDS** from the listening for each answer.*

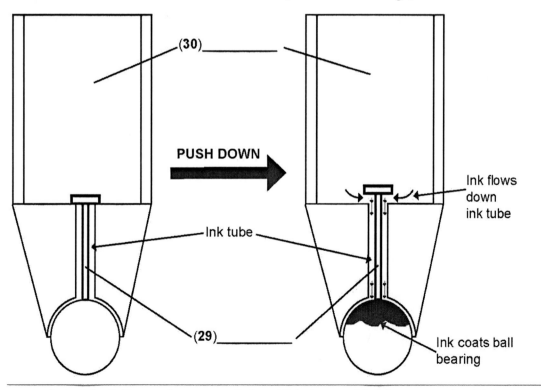

PUSH DOWN

Ink flows down ink tube

Ink tube

Ink coats ball bearing

(30)_____

(29)_____

## SECTION 4      *Questions 31 – 40*

### Questions 31 and 32

*Choose the correct letter A, B, or C.*

**31**    Domesticated rice has experienced

    **A**    the introduction of improved fertilisers in order to make it grow.
    **B**    changes at the genetic level.
    **C**    special pesticides to protect it.

**32**    The origins of domesticated rice

    **A**    are in China.
    **B**    are in India.
    **C**    are disputed.

**Questions 33 – 40**

Complete the flow chart describing the process for growing and producing rice.

Use **NO MORE THAN TWO WORDS** from the listening for each answer.

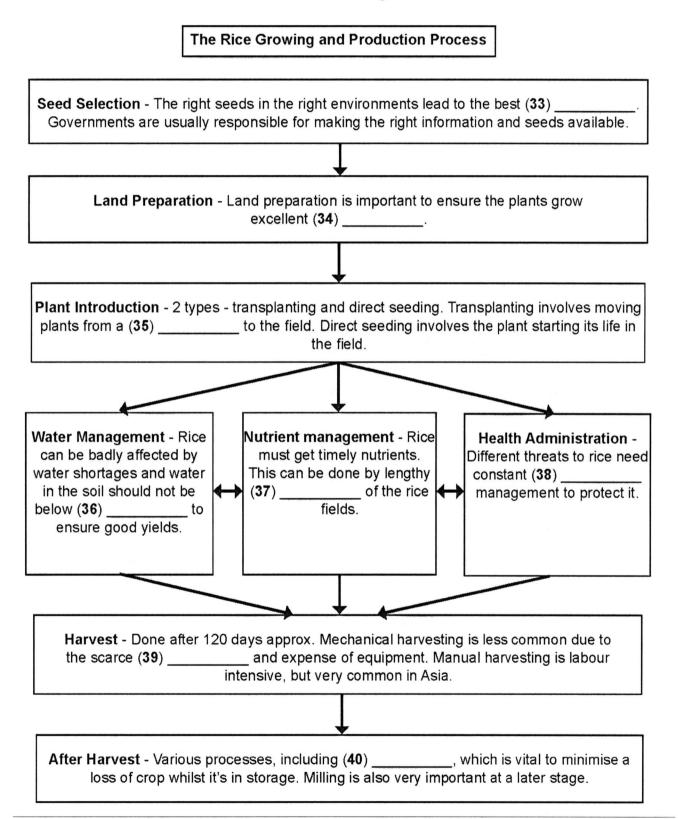

**The Rice Growing and Production Process**

**Seed Selection** - The right seeds in the right environments lead to the best (**33**) _____.
Governments are usually responsible for making the right information and seeds available.

**Land Preparation** - Land preparation is important to ensure the plants grow
excellent (**34**) _____.

**Plant Introduction** - 2 types - transplanting and direct seeding. Transplanting involves moving
plants from a (**35**) _____ to the field. Direct seeding involves the plant starting its life in
the field.

**Water Management** - Rice
can be badly affected by
water shortages and water
in the soil should not be
below (**36**) _____ to
ensure good yields.

**Nutrient management** - Rice
must get timely nutrients.
This can be done by lengthy
(**37**) _____ of the rice
fields.

**Health Administration** -
Different threats to rice need
constant (**38**) _____
management to protect it.

**Harvest** - Done after 120 days approx. Mechanical harvesting is less common due to
the scarce (**39**) _____ and expense of equipment. Manual harvesting is labour
intensive, but very common in Asia.

**After Harvest** - Various processes, including (**40**) _____, which is vital to minimise a
loss of crop whilst it's in storage. Milling is also very important at a later stage.

# READING

## SECTION 1          *Questions 1 – 14*

### *Questions 1 – 8*

*Complete the sentences below.*

Write **NO MORE THAN TWO WORDS AND/OR A NUMBER** *from the text for each answer.*

*Write your answers in boxes* **1 - 8** *on your answer sheet.*

1    _____ have different application methods and must be contacted
     directly.

2    The _____ in which people live determines which schools will give
     entrance preference.

3    Parents should apply to _____ schools in total, in case their preferred
     school does not accept their child.

4    The majority of parents submit their child's school application _____, but
     it can be done on paper if they prefer.

5    People just moving to the town should submit their proof of house purchase or
     signed _____ before a school place can be found for their child.

6    Initiating a _____ with a child's school can save unnecessary changes.

7    None of the schools' _____ can guarantee admission for any child due to
     the restrictions on resources and places.

8    _____ can require a child to be tested before they accept him/her.

## Applying to a School for your Child

If you want your child to go to a school in our town, the procedures differ slightly depending on whether you require a primary or secondary school. This system should not be used for private schools, which you should get in touch with yourself if you want to educate your child privately.

For both primary and secondary schools, which school your child can go to usually depends on where you live. Each school has a catchment area and you will get preference for entry into schools within the area where you live. For both primary and secondary school applications, you should submit an application to three educational institutions and indicate your preference in the way shown on the application form.

You need to apply for a primary school place the year before your child is due to start. Applications for both primary and secondary open on different days in each local council area, but this is usually at the start of the autumn term of the year before your child is due to start school. All children must be in education the term following their fifth birthday, so most children start when they are four. Most people apply online, but hard copy forms are also available in most pre-schools, and from the town's Children's Information Service.

For secondary schools, the application form is slightly different, as there will be a section that must be completed by your child's teacher in your child's last year in the primary school. You need to have the teacher's email address and insert it in the appropriate place on the application form. All email addresses should be available on the primary schools' websites, but it is always a good idea to contact the teacher in question to let them know before you put forward their email address.

If you have just moved to our town, you should contact the Children's Information Service for advice. We can offer a place once your contracts have been exchanged or a tenancy agreement has been signed. Places can't normally be reserved more than half a term in advance.

If your child already attends a school in our town, but you wish to move them to another within the town, then you will need to complete an application form and submit it to the Admissions Team. Before deciding on moving your child from one school to another within town, it is always a good idea to talk through the move with both the existing and new schools. Sometimes this discussion can remove the reason for the change in school.

All the school governing bodies will have done everything they can to meet the preference of parents whose applications were received by the due date in the first allocation of places within the limits of their resources. Each school has a limit on the number of pupils it can accommodate and this means that some children may not be offered a place at their preferred school, because there is no room.

All schools have admission criteria to decide which children get places. The school or local council usually set these. Admission criteria are different for each school. For example, schools may give priority to children: who have a brother or sister at the school already, who live close to the school, who do well in an entrance exam (for selective schools) or who went to a particular primary school. If a child has special educational needs, their statement of education, health and care plan will recommend a school for them. If you apply there, the school must give your child a place.

## Questions 9 – 14

*There are 4 advertisements for holiday accommodation **A – D** on the next page.*

*Which advertisement mentions the following information?*

*Write your answers in boxes **9 - 14** on your answer sheet.*

**9**      Staying at this place involves limitations on guests.

**10**     Staying at this place will get people cheaper prices at nearby restaurants.

**11**     Staying at this place involves no seasonal discounts.

**12**     Staying at this place includes a cleaner every day.

**13**     Staying at this place gives people the option to cook outside.

**14**     Staying at this place is recommended for groups.

## A        Polgeddis Cottage

Beautiful 1-bedroom cottage for rent overlooking the Green Mountains. En-suite bedroom, fully equipped kitchen, cosy living room (with open fire), maps for hiking provided with places to eat and drink marked, and discount vouchers for local eating places provided. The living room sofa is a sofa bed and so two more people can be accommodated. The property's insurance only covers four residents at any one time, so that is the maximum number of people accepted. The living room opens out onto a wooden patio where you can enjoy a drink while looking at the view and resting after a hard day's exercise. Two miles from the general store, which provides all the basics and more. There is free private parking available for up to two cars. From $600 a week, depending on the date.

## B        Downchurch Chalet

Recently refurbished and only just back on the rental market, this 3-bedroom chalet is ideal for families. Only a 3-minute walk from the beach and the safe waters of the local Atlantic bay, this chalet provides a great summer holiday. The main bedroom is for two adults and the other two will take four or five children. Two sofa beds in the living space can open out to take four more people. The kitchen is small, but well-equipped and there is a large living area. Television, DVD player and stereo are all provided, as well as a barbecue on the grass next to the chalet. The local shops and a selection of restaurants are only a 10-minute walk away. There is a spacious parking area for up to four vehicles. $900 per week in summer (July and August), $650 at other times.

## C        Salmon's Leap

For those fishing enthusiasts amongst you, Salmon's Leap is a secluded lodge near the Carbrook river. The river has a salmon run every spring and people have come from all around the world to fish its famous waters. The lodge has 5 double bedrooms, so it suits parties of people rather than 1 or 2. The kitchen is top class and there is special equipment for preparing and cooking the salmon that we hope you'll catch. There is a service visit every morning at 10 a.m., so you won't need to worry about making your bed, cleaning up the kitchen or general tidying up. A cook to prepare meals can also be arranged. Please contact us for prices and availability. The local supermarket is a 15-minute drive away and there are three good restaurants within a 20-minute drive. Check our website or independent review websites to see how visitors have loved staying with us. There is plenty of free private parking available in front of the lodge. $1500 a week during the salmon run and $1000 a week at other times.

## D        Stroudon Views

Set right in the middle of the Villamont city centre, staying at Stroudon Views will give you a starting point to see all the sites of the city. With 2 double en-suite bedrooms, this luxury apartment will give you a place to relax in the evenings after a day examining the city's museums, exhibitions or fine architecture. The apartment is situated near metro and bus stops, so getting around town couldn't be easier. The superb kitchen will allow you to prepare your own food if you don't fancy eating out, and this will give you the chance to cut back on expenses. The local neighbourhood has a variety of supermarkets, general stores, cafes and restaurants, which will satisfy all your shopping needs. The living room has comfortable sofas and armchairs, a selection of books to choose from, and has a full entertainment system, including free wifi. There is no private parking available, but there are cheap public car parks nearby. Street parking spaces are hard to find and expensive. $800 a week year round.

## SECTION 2       *Questions 15 – 27*

*Questions 15 – 21*

*Complete the summary below.*

*Write **NO MORE THAN THREE WORDS** from the text for each answer.*

*Write your answers in boxes **15 - 21** on your answer sheet.*

---

### Our Part-Time Working Scheme

The scheme permits reductions in our employees' (**15**) _____ done over chosen days. Part-time workers will get the same pay, pension, training, promotion/transfer/redundancy and career break rights. Full- and part-time workers also get the same holiday entitlement and (**16**) _____ are not counted in the leave entitlement. Workers can use (**17**) _____ with certain amounts of unused leave. Part of any final payment will be holiday pay for untaken leave. If we treat a part-time worker differently, we must show a good reason, or 'objective justification'. On written request, we will provide any reasons for our conduct with you within 21 days of receipt. (**18**) _____ of 1 month must be given for a part-time work request. All benefits (salary, terms and conditions and flexible working) will be calculated on a (**19**) _____ basis. Employees will liaise with their line manager regarding how the part-time work will be done and agreements will be recorded in writing to help resolve a potential (**20**) _____. All applications will be judged individually. Not all (**21**) _____ are eligible for part-time working, due to their requirements.

---

## Our Part-Time Working Scheme

Our part-time working scheme allows you to reduce your original contracted hours to the number of hours that suit your personal circumstances. These hours can be worked over the 5-day working week or on a certain number of days.

As stipulated in law, part-time workers will get the same treatment for:

- pay rates (including sick pay, maternity, paternity and adoption leave and pay)
- pension opportunities and benefits
- training and career development
- selection for promotion and transfer, or for redundancy
- opportunities for career breaks

In terms of holidays, part-time workers with us are also entitled to a minimum of 5.6 weeks of paid holiday each year, although this may amount to fewer actual days of paid holiday than one of our full-time workers would get. We do not include bank holidays as part of our statutory annual holiday. Both our full- and part-time workers must take at least four weeks of their statutory leave during the leave year, but we permit carry over to the next year for any leave left after that. If a part-time worker's employment ends with us, they have the right to be paid for any leave due and not taken. This will be paid at the part-time worker's employment rate and will be included in the final payment that the part-time worker receives from us. This is the same procedure for our full-time workers.

There are some situations when we don't have to treat part-time workers in the same way as full-time employees. In these situations we must be able to show there is a good reason to do so - this is called 'objective justification'. You have the right to get a written statement of reasons for your treatment by us. The request should be in writing and we must write back within 21 days.

You must provide a month's notice in advance of your wish to reduce your working week. Your annual salary will be pro-rata to the number of contracted hours worked. All terms and conditions will be pro-rata to the number of hours contracted to work. The flexible working hours scheme may apply and flexitime will be pro-rata to the number of hours contracted to work.

In consultation with your line manager, an agreement can be made on what action is taken on the hours that are reduced. For example, you may wish to reduce your hours for a short period of time only and return back to full-time after an agreed period. However, each application will be dealt with individually on its merits and will be subject to management approval and service requirements. Once an agreement has been made with your line manager, it should be put in writing and signed by both you and the appropriate manager in the Human Resources Department. This action protects both you and the company in the case of any later dispute.

Certain posts will be excluded from part-time working. These are ones that are required for a number of fixed hours per day and are required at a particular time of the day. They are listed in the Company Handbook, but the company reserves the right to add to this list at its discretion.

## Questions 22 – 27

Complete the flow chart below.

Write **NO MORE THAN TWO WORDS** from the text for each answer.

Write your answers in boxes **22 – 27** on your answer sheet.

### Starting a Business in Australia

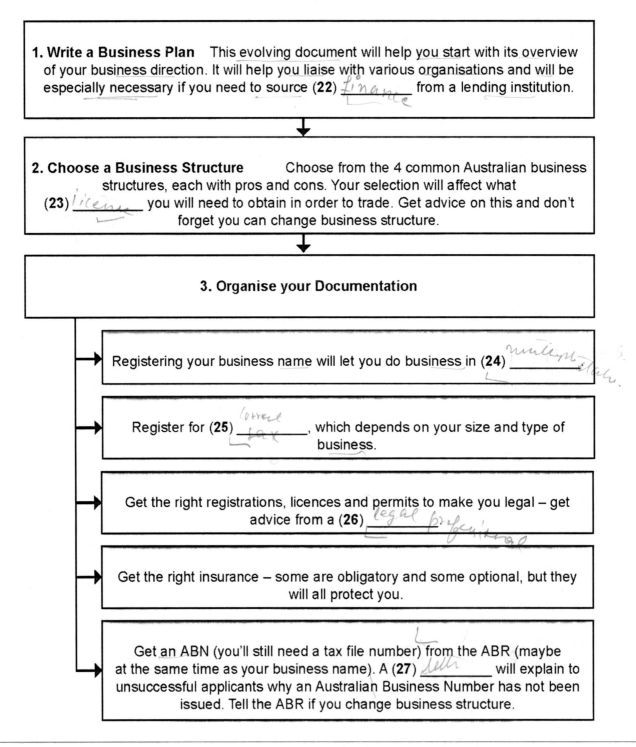

**1. Write a Business Plan**   This evolving document will help you start with its overview of your business direction. It will help you liaise with various organisations and will be especially necessary if you need to source **(22)** _finance_ from a lending institution.

**2. Choose a Business Structure**      Choose from the 4 common Australian business structures, each with pros and cons. Your selection will affect what **(23)** _licence_ you will need to obtain in order to trade. Get advice on this and don't forget you can change business structure.

**3. Organise your Documentation**

Registering your business name will let you do business in **(24)** _multiple states_

Register for **(25)** _correct tax_, which depends on your size and type of business.

Get the right registrations, licences and permits to make you legal – get advice from a **(26)** _legal professional_

Get the right insurance – some are obligatory and some optional, but they will all protect you.

Get an ABN (you'll still need a tax file number) from the ABR (maybe at the same time as your business name). A **(27)** _letter_ will explain to unsuccessful applicants why an Australian Business Number has not been issued. Tell the ABR if you change business structure.

## Do *YOU* want to start a business in Australia?

Setting up your own business can be an exciting time. Before you rent or buy premises and start trading, save yourself time and money by going through some planning and formalities.

All good businesses start with a plan. Of course, your plan will change over time, but this initial document will serve as your guide over the next three to five years. A business plan is a written document that describes your business. It covers objectives, strategies, sales, marketing and financial forecasts. It can also help to convince customers, suppliers and potential employees to support you. Banks will require one as well if you try to obtain finance from them.

You will need to choose a business structure. There are four main business structures commonly used by small businesses in Australia. These are a sole trader, a partnership, a trust or a company. When deciding upon a structure for your business, choose the one that best suits your business needs and remember that there are advantages and disadvantages for each. Choosing your business structure is an important decision that can determine the licences you will require in order to operate, so you need to investigate each option carefully. It is important to know that you're not locked into one business structure for the life of your business. As your business grows and changes, you may decide to move to a different type of business structure.

You must ensure that you have all the right documentation to run a business. You will need to register your business name if it's different from your own, and this will allow you to trade in multiple states. Business names are administered by the Australian Securities and Investments Commission (ASIC). Later, if you make changes to your business, you may also need to change your business name details. Ensuring you're registered for the correct tax is also an essential step to opening your business and this depends on the kind of business you're starting. Some registrations apply to all businesses and others may be compulsory depending on your business' size and kind. Next, having the correct registrations, licences and permits is fundamental when running your business. They allow you to operate without fear of closure from non-compliance or other legal concerns. Consulting a legal professional can help you understand your legal requirements. Finally, ensure you have all the correct insurance for your type of business. Depending on your business, there will be obligatory insurances and also some that are just advisable to have. They will protect you and your customers.

Another important formality is to obtain an Australian Business Number (ABN). An ABN is a unique eleven-digit number that identifies your business to the government and community. An ABN doesn't replace your tax file number, but it is used for various tax and other business purposes. You may apply for an ABN for free at any time through the Australian Business Register (ABR) website. Not everyone needs an ABN. To get one you need to be carrying on an enterprise. If you apply for an ABN and you're not entitled, your application may be refused. If this happens, you'll be sent a letter clarifying why. You can register for a business name at the same time as your ABN application. If you choose not to register for both at the same time you will need to go to the ASIC website to register your business name. Please note that when you change your business structure you may also be required to register a new ABN. You must inform the Australian Business Register within twenty-eight days of making any changes to your ABN registration details.

## SECTION 3      *Questions 28 - 40*

*Questions 28 – 34*

*The text on the following pages has 7 paragraphs (**A – G**).*

*Choose the correct heading for each paragraph from the list of headings below.*

*Write the correct number, **i - x**, in boxes **28 - 34** on your answer sheet.*

| | |
|---|---|
| **i** | Subsidiary Effects |
| **ii** | A Dream for the Future |
| **iii** | Enhanced Domestic Technology |
| **iv** | New Funding Offered |
| **v** | A Concentration of Power |
| **vi** | Political Pressures |
| **vii** | Working with Other Renewables |
| **viii** | A Successful Project |
| **ix** | More Technology Needed |
| **x** | Industrial Production |

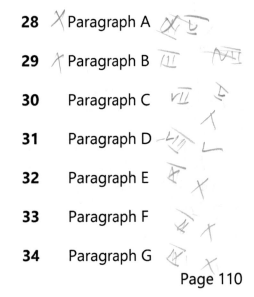

**28**   Paragraph A

**29**   Paragraph B

**30**   Paragraph C

**31**   Paragraph D

**32**   Paragraph E

**33**   Paragraph F

**34**   Paragraph G

# Solar Thermal Energy

Solar thermal energy is an important part of the much-needed energy revolution. This type of power production is safe, clean and effective and is available on the Earth every single day.

## Paragraph A

Many people associate solar power with older domestic appliances that cost a lot and only seemed to create tepid water that lasted for a few minutes. Things have moved on. Home units still use photovoltaic cells installed in solar panels, usually placed on a house's roof, but they are much improved. Modern photovoltaic cells work by having 50-micron-wide copper electrodes on the front contacts in a way that prevents diffusion of the metal, which can degrade performance. This allows incredible efficiency in exploiting any kind of sunlight, even on heavily cloudy days. This manufacturing method also adds up to a significant cost advantage when it comes to high-volume manufacturing, which is important in making the wide-scale home installation a viable commercial project. The efficient systems today might even be able to generate more power than a single house needs today if the house has enough solar panels.

## Paragraph B

Solar thermal power plants use heat from the sun to create steam, which can then be used to make electricity. Thus, these solar thermal power plants create electricity in a similar way to nuclear or coal-fired power stations and they create electricity on a scale unimagined even a generation ago. In solar thermal power plants, the heat from the sun hits a vast number of panels, which absorb the heat and transfer it to a liquid inside a tube that in turn goes to a heat exchanger. Inside the heat exchanger, the heat from the sun superheats water to create steam, which is used to spin a turbine and create the magnetic field that allows a generator to create electricity. The electricity created is then sent to the electrical grid.

## Paragraph C

The sun-rich deserts of the world play a special role, as within six hours, deserts receive more energy from the sun than humankind consumes within a year. Thanks to heat storage tanks, solar-thermal power plants in deserts can stock and supply electricity on demand twenty-four hours a day. This makes them an ideal complement to fluctuating energy sources, such as wind and photovoltaic power, and allows a higher percentage of these variable energy sources to be used in the future electricity mix.

**Paragraph D**

The Jasper Solar Thermal Farm, located near Kimberley in South Africa, was, at its time of completion, the continent's largest solar power scheme. With a rated capacity of 96 megawatts, Jasper will produce about 180,000 megawatt-hours of clean energy annually for South African residents, enough to power up to 80,000 homes. South Africa has a goal of having 18 gigawatts of renewable energy over the next 20 years, so projects like this are definitely steps in the right direction. Already the Jasper Solar Thermal Farm has been expanded by adding two further farms: the 100 megawatt Redstone Solar Thermal Power scheme and the 75 megawatt Lesedi scheme. Together the three solar projects can produce a total of 271 megawatt of generating capacity. If there's one thing that South Africa has lots of, it's sunlight!

**Paragraph E**

It's not just the production of renewable solar energy that people are attracted to. The Jasper Project, for example, generated about 1 million man-hours of paid work during construction, peaking at over 800 on-site construction jobs. Also, 45 per cent of the total project value was spent on "local content" to help increase the positive economic impact on the area. A benefit of generating electricity in desert areas is that it will not only be used for providing power for households and industry, but also to further the process of desalination, so that sea water could become drinkable. This will transform desert areas, making them potential farming zones.

**Paragraph F**

Under EU law, the European governments are obliged to reduce carbon emissions by 40 per cent over the next twenty years. EU countries are also each required to have at least 10 per cent of their transport fuels come from renewable sources over the next 10 years. The UK, for example, will cope with this by ensuring that 15 per cent of UK energy consumption comes from renewable sources, and the government has set a target for solar thermal energy production to reach 20 gigawatts, the equivalent of one traditional gas or coal-fired power station. The more southerly countries in Europe, for example Spain, can naturally exploit more solar thermal energy than others.

**Paragraph G**

In Africa's Sahara desert lie millions of square kilometres that receive a massive amount of solar energy every day. The European Commission's Institute for Energy has said that only 0.3 of the annual Sahara solar energy would be able to power the whole of Europe. Not only would this provide Europe with clean and safe energy, it would give the North African countries generating the power a large and guaranteed income, which would allow these countries to develop in ways that are not currently possible. The technology is ready, but the main stumbling block that is preventing firms that are ready to put money into the projects is the lack of political and social stability in this region. If this can be ensured, then a prosperous outlook for these countries would seem to be assured.

**Questions 35 – 37**

Label the diagram below.

Write **NO MORE THAN THREE WORDS** from the text for each answer.

Write your answers in boxes **35 - 37** on your answer sheet.

### A Solar Thermal Power Plant

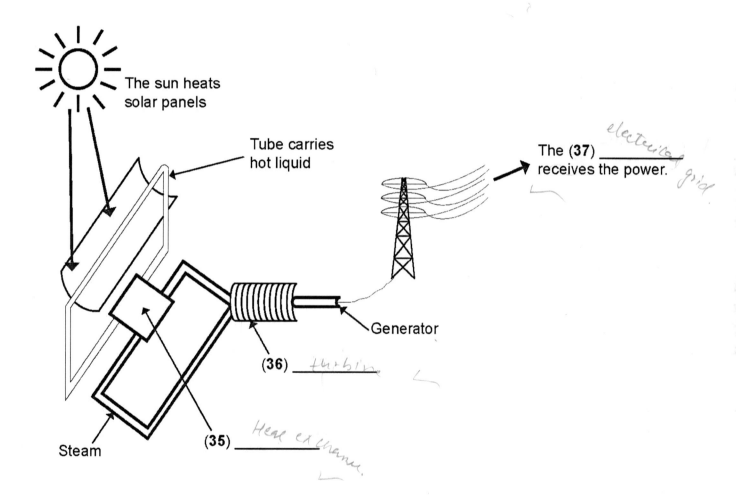

The sun heats
solar panels

Tube carries
hot liquid

The **(37)** _____
receives the power.

*electrical grid*

Generator

**(36)** _____ *turbine*

Steam

**(35)** _____ *Heat exchanger.*

**Questions 38 – 40**

*Do the following statements agree with the information given in the text?*

*In boxes 38 – 40 on your answer sheet write:*

**TRUE**            *if the statement agrees with the information*
**FALSE**           *if the statement contradicts the information*
**NOT GIVEN**       *if there is no information on this*

38     Solar thermal power plants cannot supply electricity during the night.

39     The UK has recently doubled its investment into solar thermal energy.

40     At the moment, few companies are willing to invest in North African solar energy.

# WRITING

## WRITING TASK 1

*You should spend about 20 minutes on this task.*

> **You recently received a letter from your bank that should have contained a new credit card. Unfortunately, the card was not in the letter.**
>
> **Write a letter to your bank manager. In your letter,**
>
> - **explain what has happened**
> - **suggest the credit card should be cancelled for security reasons**
> - **ask when a new credit card can be sent to you**

*You should write at least 150 words.*

*You do **NOT** need to write any addresses. Begin your letter as follows:*

> ***Dear Sir / Madam,***

## WRITING TASK 2

*You should spend about 40 minutes on this task.*

*Write about the following topic:*

> **There is a problem today that copyright materials such as music, films and books are freely available on the internet with the result that the owners of the works lose money.**
>
> **Do you feel that this is a good or bad thing?**

*Give reasons for your answer and include any relevant examples from your knowledge or experience.*

*You should write at least 250 words.*

# SPEAKING

## SECTION 1

- Can you describe a school that you have attended?
- How do you feel this school could be improved?
- Do you still keep in touch with friends from school? (Why/Why not?)

Topic 1      Job Interviews
- How do/would you prepare for a job interview?
- What kinds of questions do you think a good interviewer would ask in a job interview?
- How would you dress for a job interview?
- How would you convince someone to give you a job?

Topic 2      Music
- What kinds of music do you like?
- Why do people like to listen to music?
- What advantages are there to learning to play a musical instrument?
- Why do some people particularly like to listen to live music?

## SECTION 2

Describe a memorable visit to the doctor or to a hospital
You should say:
        why you were there
        how long you were there
        what happened while you were there
and explain why this visit was particularly memorable.

## SECTION 3

Topic 1      Doctors and Nurses
- What qualities do you think are important for a good doctor and a good nurse?
- Do you think that doctors are overpaid for what they do? (Why/Why not?)
- Why do doctors hold such respect in most societies?
- How do you think the role of a doctor will change in the future?

Topic 2      Health Services
- Do you feel that your country has good health services? (Why/Why not?)
- Do you think that people should pay for their country's health services or should they be free?
- How have your country's health services changed over the last 20 years?
- What do you think have been the major advances in medicine over the last hundred years?

## Listening Test Answer Sheet

| | | | |
|---|---|---|---|
| 1 | | 21 | |
| 2 | | 22 | |
| 3 | | 23 | |
| 4 | | 24 | |
| 5 | | 25 | |
| 6 | | 26 | |
| 7 | | 27 | |
| 8 | | 28 | |
| 9 | | 29 | |
| 10 | | 30 | |
| 11 | | 31 | |
| 12 | | 32 | |
| 13 | | 33 | |
| 14 | | 34 | |
| 15 | | 35 | |
| 16 | | 36 | |
| 17 | | 37 | |
| 18 | | 38 | |
| 19 | | 39 | |
| 20 | | 40 | |

## Reading Test Answer Sheet

| | | | |
|---|---|---|---|
| 1 | | 21 | |
| 2 | | 22 | |
| 3 | | 23 | |
| 4 | | 24 | |
| 5 | | 25 | |
| 6 | | 26 | |
| 7 | | 27 | |
| 8 | | 28 | |
| 9 | | 29 | |
| 10 | | 30 | |
| 11 | | 31 | |
| 12 | | 32 | |
| 13 | | 33 | |
| 14 | | 34 | |
| 15 | | 35 | |
| 16 | | 36 | |
| 17 | | 37 | |
| 18 | | 38 | |
| 19 | | 39 | |
| 20 | | 40 | |

# Answers

# LISTENING ANSWERS

/ indicates an alternative answer          ( ) indicates an optional answer

| TEST 6 | TEST 7 | TEST 8 | TEST 9 | TEST 10 |
|---|---|---|---|---|
| 1. Colin | 1. B | 1. Melissa | 1. Castle | 1. 2 |
| 2. 15 | 2. C | 2. 30 | 2. 30th/30 | 2. $1000 / a thousand dollars |
| 3. JU 731 | 3. B | 3. cinema | 3. Australia | 3. (the) kitchen |
| 4. Premium (policy) | 4. A | 4. 11,000 | 4. 443 | 4. (the) (garden's) maintenance |
| 5. 462 | 5. A | 5. 14 nights | 5. 2 hours | 5. 2 months' rent |
| 6. A* | 6. B* | 6. flights | 6. scans | 6. renovated |
| 7. C* | 7. D* | 7. Lectures | 7. train | 7. deposit |
| 8. D* | 8. E* | 8. (Travel) insurance | 8. part-time/part time | 8. living room |
| 9. F* | 9. G* | 9. 9,000 | 9. (personal) relationships | 9. (school) bus |
| 10. H* | 10. I* | 10. (Swimming) pool | 10. commission | 10. Combined |
| 11. C | 11. vegetables | 11. low income | 11. 7000 | 11. E |
| 12. G | 12. export | 12. hospitals | 12. photo ID | 12. J |
| 13. B | 13. competition | 13. website | 13. blood sample | 13. B* |
| 14. D | 14. holiday (in Scotland) | 14. 1/a dollar | 14. email | 14. C* |
| 15. F | 15. children | 15. immigrant | 15. 8 | 15. E* |
| 16. 10 (p.m.) | 16. C | 16. B | 16. public holidays | 16. G |
| 17. (A) garage | 17. E | 17. A | 17. travel (risk) form | 17. A |
| 18. (On) (the) beach | 18. A | 18. C | 18. (At) reception | 18. C |
| 19. (The) town centre | 19. B | 19. D | 19. (The) (practice) manager | 19. D |
| 20. (A) taxi | 20. D | 20. G | 20. (The) (practice) offices | 20. F |
| 21. Europe | 21. B | 21. oil prices | 21. B | 21. B |
| 22. (work) permit | 22. A | 22. Citation(s) | 22. A | 22. F |
| 23. grammar | 23. C | 23. (guidance) sheet | 23. C | 23. A |
| 24. cafés/cafes | 24. B | 24. immigration | 24. B | 24. G |
| 25. quality | 25. C | 25. revision | 25. C | 25. E |
| 26. Arabic | 26. N | 26. A | 26. F | 26. A |
| 27. vocabulary | 27. K | 27. B | 27. H | 27. A |
| 28. approved programme / approved program | 28. C | 28. B | 28. I | 28. B |
| 29. contacts | 29. (confirmation) letter | 29. A | 29. B | 29. (a) (central) spring |
| 30. translation | 30. password | 30. C | 30. E | 30. (the) ink (tank) |
| 31. move | 31. Social | 31. D | 31. condensation | 31. B |
| 32. 10th | 32. Teenagers | 32. C | 32. cool | 32. C |
| 33. (flammable) properties | 33. bones | 33. F | 33. formation (processes) | 33. yields |
| 34. (nasty) fumes | 34. hyperactivity | 34. E | 34. (barren) hills | 34. root systems |
| 35. friction | 35. sugar | 35. A | 35. medical purposes | 35. nursery |
| 36. danger | 36. (low-fat) milk | 36. obsolete | 36. monopoly | 36. saturation |
| 37. self-lighting | 37. machines | 37. (physical) mark | 37. copper | 37. flooding |
| 38. striking surface | 38. moderation | 38. framework | 38. scientists | 38. pest |
| 39. (Harmless) charcoal | 39. role models | 39. equal treatment | 39. (delicate) balance | 39. availability |
| 40. (Orange) flame | 40. (careful) education | 40. (legal) verification | 40. growth (cycles) | 40. drying |
| **Note:** Answers for qu. 6, 7, 8, 9 and 10 can be written in any order. | **Note:** Answers for qu. 6, 7, 8, 9 and 10 can be written in any order. | | | **Note:** Answers for qu. 11, 12 and 13 can be written in any order. |

# READING ANSWERS

/ indicates an alternative answer          ( ) indicates an optional answer

| TEST 6 | TEST 7 | TEST 8 | TEST 9 | TEST 10 |
|---|---|---|---|---|
| 1. C | 1. B | 1. (For) 20 years | 1. Lessons | 1. Private schools |
| 2. D | 2. A | 2. (Their) postcode | 2. guides | 2. (catchment) area |
| 3. E | 3. C | 3. (A) password | 3. life vests | 3. 3 |
| 4. A | 4. D | 4. Debit cards | 4. refreshments | 4. online |
| 5. G | 5. F | 5. Twice a year | 5. benches | 5. (tenancy) agreement |
| 6. F | 6. A | 6. (Our) carbon footprint | 6. (information) boards | 6. discussion |
| 7. B | 7. (any) (formal) action | 7. (Local) (organic) farms | 7. (Weather) forecast / Weather | 7. governing bodies |
| 8. TRUE | 8. (complaints) procedures | 8. long-term investment | 8. v | 8. (Selective) schools |
| 9. FALSE | 9. 8 weeks | 9. (tax) rebates | 9. vii | 9. A |
| 10. NOT GIVEN | 10. binding | 10. credentials | 10. iii | 10. A |
| 11. FALSE | 11. tariffs | 11. warranty | 11. vi | 11. D |
| 12. NOT GIVEN | 12. (price) (comparison) websites | 12. FALSE | 12. ii | 12. C |
| 13. TRUE | 13. contract | 13. NOT GIVEN | 13. ix | 13. B |
| 14. TRUE | 14. penalty | 14. TRUE | 14. iv | 14. C |
| 15. (The) (bar) code | 15. C | 15. subsidies | 15. contract | 15. (original) (contracted) hours |
| 16. (Considerable) discounts | 16. B | 16. (permanent) job | 16. probation (period) | 16. bank holidays |
| 17. Unlimited (numbers) | 17. F | 17. (local) colleges | 17. (A) notice | 17. carry over |
| 18. Fuel (price) (fluctuations) / (Fuel) price (fluctuations) | 18. D | 18. (qualified) tradesperson | 18. (self-evaluation) statement | 18. (A) notice |
| 19. E-mail | 19. C | 19. Study leave | 19. informal | 19. pro-rata |
| 20. Recommendations | 20. A | 20. rewarding | 20. Rating | 20. dispute |
| 21. receipt | 21. E | 21. website | 21. tab | 21. posts |
| 22. reception | 22. expansion | 22. unreasonable | 22. impractical | 22. finance |
| 23. Swipe | 23. headhunter (firm) | 23. unfair | 23. dynamic | 23. licences |
| 24. waiver | 24. email | 24. employment tribunal | 24. discriminatory | 24. multiple states |
| 25. (social) (engineering) techniques | 25. suitability | 25. (disciplinary) rules | 25. (privacy) settings | 25. tax |
| 26. passwords | 26. back-up | 26. claim | 26. (work-life) balance | 26. (legal) professional |
| 27. visitors' policy | 27. report | 27. (full) pay | 27. (New) opportunities | 27. letter |
| 28. ii | 28. iii | 28. GR | 28. JG | 28. iii |
| 29. vii | 29. vi | 29. KC | 29. TC | 29. x |
| 30. iv | 30. i | 30. DS | 30. JH | 30. v |
| 31. x | 31. iv | 31. AK | 31. PC | 31. viii |
| 32. v | 32. viii | 32. KC | 32. JG | 32. i |
| 33. i | 33. v | 33. WG | 33. JH | 33. vi |
| 34. viii | 34. TRUE | 34. GR | 34. JB | 34. ii |
| 35. NO | 35. TRUE | 35. C | 35. JH | 35. (A) heat exchanger |
| 36. YES | 36. FALSE | 36. A | 36. FALSE | 36. (A) turbine |
| 37. YES | 37. NOT GIVEN | 37. C | 37. TRUE | 37. electrical grid |
| 38. NOT GIVEN | 38. B | 38. B | 38. FALSE | 38. FALSE |
| 39. Enzymes | 39. D | 39. water table | 39. NOT GIVEN | 39. NOT GIVEN |
| 40. carbon dioxide | 40. E | 40. (deeper) aquifer | 40. B | 40. TRUE |

# READING ANSWERS HELP

This section shows fragments of passages that contain the correct answers. If you have trouble locating the correct answer in the text, or can't understand why a particular answer is correct, refer to this section to understand the reasoning behind the answers. A group of answers with answers being preceded by * means that this group of answers may be given in any order. Answers in brackets () are optional answers.

## GENERAL READING TEST 6

1. **C**            No reservations, just turn up.

2. **D**            The Aloha offers you dormitory style accommodation

3. **E**            Major city centre hotel requires a smart and multi-skilled person for reception duty.

4. **A**            *Consult our website for availability, prices and special offers!*

5. **G**            Call one of our salespeople, so we can visit your premises or discuss things on the phone.

6. **F**            Bring and pitch your own tent or rent one of our self-catering cabins (capacity 5).

7. **B**            Nestling on the sea shore

8. **TRUE**            Arena has easy access from different roads for drivers

9. **FALSE**            Open every Sunday, from 15th March to 15th December, rain, shine or snow!

10. **NOT GIVEN**            There is nothing in the text relating to this and so the answer is 'not given' in the text.

11. **FALSE**            No lorries, please!

12. **NOT GIVEN**            There is nothing in the text relating to this and so the answer is 'not given' in the text.

13. **TRUE**            sellers welcome as many questions as you feel necessary

14. **TRUE**            At the same time, be careful of pickpockets in the crowds when carrying your items around.

15. **(The) (bar) code**            The bar code on the label will be scanned every time your package is moved, and in this way you can track your package 24 hours a day and know exactly where it is and what its status is.

16. **(Considerable) discounts**        considerable discounts on national and international pick-ups and deliveries when 50 letters or packages are passed.

17. **Unlimited (numbers)**             Unlimited numbers of letters and packages of weight up to 20 kilograms

18. **Fuel (price) fluctuations / (Fuel) price (fluctuations)**        Prices vary considerably due to fuel price fluctuations

19. **E-mail**      Send an e-mail to our Customer Services department via the contact details listed.

20. **Recommendations**        *Check our website for recommendations from hundreds of satisfied businesses in your area.*

21. **receipt**      First, we require a passport sized digital photo for your company ID card. Please email us one as soon as possible. If you have to pay for one, please retain the receipt, so that you can be reimbursed.

22. **reception**         When you arrive for your first day at work, please go to reception. They will be expecting you and will issue you with your ID card.

23. **Swipe**      After you receive your ID card and every time you enter or leave the company building, please swipe your card on the reader at the entrance. The reader is at chest level for people who already have the cards around their necks. The swiping of your card allows the company to track your working hours, so that they can correctly assess any overtime or flexitime that you do. It also allows the company to know who is in the building at any one time

24. **waiver**      During it, you will be asked to endorse a waiver, allowing us to monitor your movements around the building on our CCTV system and your movements on the Internet.

25. **(social) (engineering) techniques**         Various social engineering techniques can also be used to gather secret information or extract credentials from employees. Random USB sticks, left in a hallway for curious employees to pick up and use, or carefully written emails that prompt clicking on a link, are only two of a large number of ways through which malware can infect our systems, giving competitors full access to sensitive data.

26. **passwords**        After your security briefing, please go to the IT department on the 3rd floor. The IT people will assign you all the passwords that you will need to operate our systems.

27. **visitors' policy**         Finally, on return to your department, you will be asked to read and initial our visitors' policy.

28. **ii**         Various information within Paragraph A.

29. **vii**        Various information within Paragraph B.

30. **iv**          Various information within Paragraph C.

31. **x**           Various information within Paragraph D.

32. **v**           Various information within Paragraph E.

33. **i**           Various information within Paragraph F.

34. **viii**        Various information within Paragraph G.

35. **NO**          In contrast to the UK, artisan bakeries still dominate the market in many mainland European countries.

36. **YES**         This early bread was particularly successful, when wild yeast from the air combined with the flour and water.

37. **YES**         The Romans preferred whiter bread, which was possible with the milling processes that they had refined. This led to white bread being perceived as the most valuable bread of them all, a preference that seems to have stuck with many people.

38. **NOT GIVEN**       There is nothing in the text relating to this and so the answer is 'not given' in the text.

39. **Enzymes**         The basics of any bread dough are flour, water, and of course, yeast. As soon as these ingredients are stirred together, enzymes in the yeast and the flour cause large starch molecules to break down into simple sugars.

40. **carbon dioxide**          The yeast metabolises these simple sugars and exudes a fluid that releases carbon dioxide into the dough's minute cells. As more and more tiny cells are filled, the dough rises and leavened bread is the result.

## GENERAL READING TEST 7

1. **B**          Discounts available if booked on our website.

2. **A**          Monthly payment options

3. **C**          Cleaners fully insured

4. **D**          Our country-wide network guarantees to get to you within 60 minutes of your call, with a female priority service in action.

5. **F**          For over 30 years, I have been restoring classic cars for clients around the world.

6. **A**          Free courtesy car included during repairs

7. **(any) (formal) action**     Before starting any formal action, you should contact the energy company directly.

8. **(complaints) procedures**        All companies are required to deal proactively with complaints from domestic consumers and they all have mandatory complaints procedures detailing how they do this.

9. **8 weeks**    The Ombudsman Services in charge of Energy (OSE) can investigate if the complaint hasn't been resolved to your satisfaction at the end of eight weeks.

10. **binding**    The OSE can require the company to correct the problem, apologise, explain what happened, and make a financial award. Its decisions are binding on the energy company, but not the consumer.

11. **tariffs**    If you do decide to change, make sure you compare energy tariffs and deals regularly

12. **(price) (comparison) websites**        There are a number of price comparison websites available at the present time and these can offer disinterested and simple sources of advice.

13. **contract**   You will agree over the phone and the contract will arrive in the post.

14. **penalty**    After this timeframe, there may be a penalty to exit depending on what has been agreed upon.

15. **C**          Don't answer the phone when there are waiting customers

16. **B**          Look as though you're happy that the customer has come into your shop or restaurant

17. **F**          never swear and don't talk about customers in front of other customers.

18. **D**          Stay calm, don't take anything to heart and be polite, no matter what the customer says

Page 124

19. **C**          Don't allow a talkative customer to take up too much of your time when others are waiting.

20. **A**          It's usually fine to be less formal with younger people, but older customers often don't appreciate being called "you guys" or similar. Use your common sense, and be polite. Remember, no one objects to being called "sir" or "madam"!

21. **E**          check the goods when you're packing them to make sure they have what they paid for

22. **expansion**          The first step in the recruitment process is to decide if your organisation needs a new employee. The need might come from someone leaving the company or increased business activity or scheduled expansion.

23. **headhunter (firm)**          The advertisement for the vacancy needs to be posted in appropriate places. A headhunter firm might be used if the vacancy warrants it.

24. **email**          The committee should create a short list and contact unsuccessful applicants. A short email will suffice.

25. **suitability**          The interviews should be conducted by the selection committee. They should have questions and/or tasks ready. Although questions will normally be related to the job description, the committee may want to include various questions that stretch and surprise the candidate to test his/her suitability.

26. **back-up**          The selection committee will assess the second interviewees and choose a successful candidate and a back-up in case the job offer is refused.

27. **report**          finally a report should be written for the appropriate managers, the human resources department and for the employee's file.

28. **iii**          Various information within Paragraph A.

29. **vi**          Various information within Paragraph B.

30. **i**          Various information within Paragraph C.

31. **iv**          Various information within Paragraph D.

32. **viii**          Various information within Paragraph E.

33. **v**          Various information within Paragraph F.

34. **TRUE**          it appears that China had less use for the kind of accurate timekeeping that came to rule the West

35. **TRUE**     The first mechanical clock probably emerged out of monasteries, developed by monks as alarm mechanisms to ring the bells according to the regular and regimented hours of their rituals.

36. **FALSE**     Early watches were bulky and ornate and, like the early spring-powered clocks, kept time with only an hour hand, though still rather imprecisely due to errors from friction.

37. **NOT GIVEN**     There is nothing in the text relating to this and so the answer is 'not given' in the text.

38. **B**     This, poor transportation and communication among participants in the British watch industry led to them losing their market dominance.

39. **D**     Gradually, improvements in battery technology, the miniaturisation of batteries, additional components combined with quartz technology and integrated circuit technology combined to produce the most accurate timepieces ever assembled.

40. **E**     but the Japanese were the best at controlling their distribution channels.

## GENERAL READING TEST 8

1. **(For) 20 years**      We've been growing and selling organic fruit and vegetables on our farm now for twenty years

2. **(Their) postcode**        Customers should go to our website and put their postcode into our rangefinder to see how much it is to get our products to them.

3. **(A) password**      All you need to give us is your email address and of course a password.

4. **Debit cards**        Credit cards are subject to a small fee dependent on the type of card, but debit cards are free.

5. **Twice a year**      We have open days twice a year

6. **(Our) carbon footprint**      First of all, we try and buy from producers as close to us as possible, which cuts down on our carbon footprint.

7. **(Local) (organic) farms**             we also have regular deliveries of fresh dairy products and eggs from local organic farms.

8. **long-term investment**      Solar panels are a long-term investment in your home; you want them to last.

9. **(tax) rebates**      A qualified, experienced installer not only designs your solar panels, but can also save you money by guiding you through the process of securing tax rebates and financing options.

10. **credentials**      It's important to choose an installer who has the correct credentials and who is a member of the right professional bodies.

11. **warranty**        And don't forget the warranty - solar panels are constantly exposed to the elements and can degrade if not of sufficient quality; you need to ensure your protection.

12. **FALSE**      Employees will not be notified about the dates and times of the fire evacuation practices.

13. **NOT GIVEN**        There is nothing in the text relating to this and so the answer is 'not given' in the text.

14. **TRUE**      All windows and doors should be shut (but not locked) when people are evacuating the building.

15. **subsidies**        In order to sustain the supply of skilled craftsmen, the government has offered Bowman's subsidies in order to train apprentices.

16. **(permanent) job**        Successful apprentices might find a permanent job with us or maybe they will go out and start their own business.

17. **(local) colleges**        Our apprenticeships are carried out in partnership with local colleges and your training will include classroom as well as building site time.

18. **(qualified) tradesperson**        Each apprentice will be allocated a qualified tradesperson.

19. **Study leave**        You may also be able to take some time off for study leave in addition to your usual paid leave

20. **rewarding**        Your apprenticeship will be very rewarding, even if at times it may seem demanding.

21. **website**        In order to apply for an apprenticeship with us, you will need to visit our website (www.bowmansbuilding.com).

22. **unreasonable**        This could be because of a variety of reasons, including the cause the employer gave for the dismissal wasn't the real one, the reason the employer gave was unfair or the employer was unreasonable in their actions

23. **unfair**     A constructive dismissal isn't necessarily unfair, but it would be difficult for an employer to show that a breach of contract was fair.

24. **employment tribunal**        If an employee thinks an employer has dismissed them unfairly, constructively or wrongfully, the employee might take the employer to an employment tribunal.

25. **(disciplinary) rules**        What an organisation regards as this kind of misbehaviour should be clear from its disciplinary rules.

26. **claim**     Failing to establish the facts before taking action and holding a meeting with the employee, and denying the employee the right to appeal is highly likely to be considered unfair and lead to a claim against the employer.

27. **(full) pay**        For any dismissal, It may not be appropriate for the employee to be at work while facts are established, so a short period of suspension on full pay may be helpful.

28. **GR**        Ronaldson continues to justify the approach. "The use of relevant technologies is important, as in many places around the world, water provision efforts suffer from a lack of technical knowledge to effectively manage or adapt a system to a community's fluctuating needs."

29. **KC**        As Kathie Coles, an executive from the charity World of Water, describes, the situation will deteriorate. "Over the next 20 years, an estimated 1.8 billion people will be living in countries or regions with an absolute water scarcity, and two-thirds of the world population may be under stress conditions. This situation will only worsen, as rapidly growing urban areas place heavy pressure on water supplies."

30. **DS**        Darren Stanford, a water quality engineer, explains the important three-step methodology … The third is the evaluation of the impact of the interventions on the health and quality of life of the consumers."

31. **AK**        Alex Karpov, a representative from the World Health Organisation, explains some of the other issues that also impact the availability of fresh water. "The deterioration of ground water and surface water quality, competition for water between different segments of society, for example, between agricultural, industrial, and domestic users, and even social and financial barriers, are all causes of water stress and scarcity today."

32. **KC**        As Kathie Coles, an executive from the charity World of Water, describes, the situation will deteriorate. "Over the next 20 years, an estimated 1.8 billion people will be living in countries or regions with an absolute water scarcity, and two-thirds of the world population may be under stress conditions.

33. **WG**        Will Goodman, a doctor with the World Health Organisation, says that this can affect communities in different ways. "The emergence of the adult female worm can be very painful, slow, and disabling and prevents people from working in their fields, tending their animals, going to school, and caring for their families."

34. **GR**        Georgina Ronaldson, a spokesperson for the World Bank, recently announced a way to deal with current difficulties. "To help developing countries, various concerned organisations have developed the Safe Water System (SWS), which is an adaptable and flexible intervention that employs scientific methods appropriate for the developing world."

35. **C**        Of the accessible fresh water supplies, nearly 70 per cent is withdrawn and used for irrigation to produce food

36. **A**        Of course, there have been different initiatives put into place around the world to help with water stress and scarcity. While larger scale projects, such as the construction of piped water systems, remain important objectives of many development agencies, a shortage of time and finances will leave hundreds of millions of people without access to safe water in the foreseeable future.

37. **C**        Darren Stanford, a water quality engineer, explains the important three-step methodology. "The first is an assessment of the water delivery system from catchment to consumer.

38. **B**        The eradication efforts make use of simple interventions for providing safe drinking water

39. **water table**        Many existing dug wells in communities only pierce the topsoil, do not reach deep enough and are therefore readily influenced by drought or by the natural declines from summer to autumn in the water table.

40. **(deeper) aquifer**        SWS borehole wells can pierce the bedrock and access a deeper aquifer with water that is not affected by surface drought. These are also unaffected by guinea worm infestation and the water is much safer for human consumption.

## GENERAL READING TEST 9

1. **Lessons**                You can get lessons for yourself and/or your child

2. **guides**        or you can take a guided trek into the local forests and hills. You'll be taken for up to four hours around the local area to see the wonderful countryside and hopefully lots of the local animals. There are various sights to take in, such as castles, and John's guides know the area well and exactly where to go.

3. **life vests**    We'll take you to a good starting point on the river and give you a map, so you know where you're going. For safety, there are life vests provided and we'll give you some hints on kayaking.

4. **refreshments**        We have plenty of maps of the trails and advice on places to pause for refreshments.

5. **benches**            It's been eroding all that time, so it's not that difficult a climb and there are well-tended paths with benches on which to take a break.

6. **(information) boards**      In addition, there are lots of information boards scattered around, so that you can learn about the formation of the volcano and its history.

7. **(Weather) forecast / Weather**          *As you can see, lots of our activities are outside, so make sure you inform yourself regarding the weather forecast to avoid getting too wet (if that bothers you!).*

8. **v**        Various information within Section A.

9. **vii**        Various information within Section B.

10. **iii**        Various information within Section C.

11. **vi**        Various information within Section D.

12. **ii**        Various information within Section E.

13. **ix**        Various information within Section F.

14. **iv**        Various information within Section G.

15. **contract**        The job description will have outlined the roles and responsibilities of the employee's position. The contract will then stipulate these things officially.

16. **probation (period)**        although there will be a 3-month review of the employee at the conclusion of the probation period. The three-month review allows both employer and employee to be sure that their commitment to each other is warranted.

Page 130

**17. (A) notice** Before the annual meeting, the employee should receive at least two weeks' notice.

**18. (self-evaluation) statement** The employee should give a self-evaluation statement to the manager(s) conducting the meeting giving his/her views of his/her performance over the year in terms of the roles and responsibilities.

**19. informal** There should be plenty of time allocated to the appraisal meeting. It should be reasonably informal, so that the employee is at ease and can discuss his/her performance without any undue pressure.

**20. Rating** At the end of the meeting, there will be a rating of the employee's performance.

**21. tab** Employees should consult the company handbook to inform themselves about this process. This can be located under the appropriate tab on the company Intranet or in a hard copy format at reception or with any of the line managers.

**22. impractical** However, it might prove impractical to have an overly formal policy that also includes rigidly covering the use of social media in recruitment.

**23. dynamic** While a rigid policy on using social media in recruitment could soon become obsolete, because the trend is so dynamic

**24. discriminatory** In particular when recruiting, employers should be careful if they assess applicants by looking at their social networking pages, as this may be discriminatory.

**25. (privacy) settings** Employees should regularly review the privacy settings on their social networking pages, as they can change. Also, they should consider whether they want or need co-workers to see those profiles.

**26. (work-life) balance** Employers should promote a work-life balance - the line between work and home is becoming increasingly blurred by the use of modern technology.

**27. (New) opportunities** If you try to be too specific, you may find the policy needs updating every few months just to stay relevant. + It's also important you don't impede your staff from exploring new opportunities in social media.

**28. JG** Jim Gagliano, Jockey Club President, reported on the effects of the drop in numbers on the horse racing industry. "The thoroughbred foal crop has been declining and is responsible for a drop in the number of starts, number of horses in the field, the number of owners, and the number of racing days. This in turn has led to a drop in turnover for all sectors in the industry and makes the industry a less attractive one for fresh entrants and existing businesses."

**29. TC** Capps pointed out the horse industry often parallels the wider economy and the current situation closely mirrors the impact the Great Depression had on the industry.

30. **JH**          said AHC president Jay Hickey. "It was a very good program and attendees now have a better comprehension of current conditions and what actions are being taken."

31. **PC**          Following up on the need for more and better marketing, Patti Colbert of PCE Enterprises has come up with the *Time to Ride* initiative. This ambitious national campaign and contest targets the goal of giving 100,000 new people a horse experience in the following calendar year. Ms. Colbert reported that *Time to Ride* had accomplished its initial goal to sign up 1,000 stables, instructors, new participants and others in the horse community to host events.

32. **JG**          Mr. Gagliano said that institutions are working to promote the best races and make better use of social media and online resources to attract a younger demographic, and develop new owners.

33. **JH**          Hickey explains why people are not overly worried just yet. "The industry also has one great advantage: the enduring appeal of the horse. With continued effort on the part of the entire horse community, the industry will come out of the current economic climate even more robust."

34. **JB**          Blea additionally spoke about the AAEP programs to help veterinarians create long-term and successful relationships with horse owners and support an increase in horse breeding.

35. **JH**          Hickey explains why stakeholders are not overly worried just yet. "The horse business also has one great advantage: the enduring appeal of the horse.

36. **FALSE**       The industrial revolution and in particular the invention of the internal combustion engine was the end of the horse's central role in people's lives.

37. **TRUE**        Capps also noted that this is not the first such decline in the number of horses, and in previous instances there was later a strong rebound in numbers.

38. **FALSE**       Tim Capps, Director of the Equine Industry Program at the University of Louisville, gave the opening address at the forum and tried to pinpoint the reasons for the drop in today's numbers of registered horses. The economy was cited by Capps as the single largest factor, but there are probably several other factors as well. Capps believes the horse industry was in a bubble that peaked about six years before, which was similar to an earlier bubble in the 1980's.

39. **NOT GIVEN**        There is nothing in the text relating to this and so the answer is 'not given' in the text.

40. **B**          This is a holistic answer and involves synthesis of the whole text. This text in its entirety fits "To review initiatives addressing current challenges to the horse industry." better than the other three answers.

## GENERAL READING TEST 10

1. **Private schools**         This system should not be used for private schools, which you should get in touch with yourself if you want to educate your child privately.

2. **(catchment) area**         For both primary and secondary schools, which school your child can go to usually depends on where you live. Each school has a catchment area and you will get preference for entry into schools within the area where you live.

3. **3**         For both primary and secondary school applications, you should submit an application to three educational institutions and indicate your preference in the way shown on the application form.

4. **online**         Most people apply online, but hard copy forms are also available in most pre-schools, and from the town's Children's Information Service.

5. **(tenancy) agreement**         We can offer a place once your contracts have been exchanged or a tenancy agreement has been signed.

6. **discussion**         Before deciding on moving your child from one school to another within town, it is always a good idea to talk through the move with both the existing and new schools. Sometimes this discussion can remove the reason for the change in school.

7. **governing bodies**         All the school governing bodies will have done everything they can to meet the preference of parents whose applications were received by the due date in the first allocation of places within the limits of their resources. Each school has a limit on the number of pupils it can accommodate and this means that some children may not be offered a place at their preferred school, because there is no room.

8. **(Selective) schools**         For example, schools may give priority to children: who have a brother or sister at the school already, who live close to the school, who do well in an entrance exam (for selective schools)

9. **A**         The property's insurance only covers four residents at any one time, so that is the maximum number of people accepted.

10. **A**         discount vouchers for local eating places provided.

11. **D**         $800 a week year round.

12. **C**         There is a service visit every morning at 10 a.m., so you won't need to worry about making your bed, cleaning up the kitchen or general tidying up.

13. **B**         as well as a barbecue on the grass next to the chalet.

14. **C**         The lodge has 5 double bedrooms, so it suits parties of people rather than 1 or 2.

**15. (original) (contracted) hours**          Our part-time working scheme allows you to reduce your original contracted hours to the number of hours that suit your personal circumstances.

**16. bank holidays**          We do not include bank holidays as part of our statutory annual holiday.

**17. carry over**          Both our full- and part-time workers must take at least four weeks of their statutory leave during the leave year, but we permit carry over to the next year for any leave left after that.

**18. (A) notice**          You must provide a month's notice in advance of your wish to reduce your working week.

**19. pro-rata**          All terms and conditions will be pro-rata to the number of hours contracted to work.

**20. dispute**          Once an agreement has been made with your line manager, it should be put in writing and signed by both you and the appropriate manager in the Human Resources Department. This action protects both you and the company in the case of any later dispute.

**21. posts**          Certain posts will be excluded from part-time working. These are ones that are required for a number of fixed hours per day and are required at a particular time of the day.

**22. finance**          Banks will require one as well if you try to obtain finance from them.

**23. licences**          Choosing your business structure is an important decision that can determine the licences you will require in order to operate

**24. multiple states**          You will need to register your business name if it's different from your own, and this will allow you to trade in multiple states.

**25. tax**          Ensuring you're registered for the correct tax is also an essential step to opening your business and this depends on the kind of business you're starting. Some registrations apply to all businesses and others may be compulsory depending on your business' size and kind.

**26. (legal) professional**          Next, having the correct registrations, licences and permits is fundamental when running your business. They allow you to operate without fear of closure from non-compliance or other legal concerns. Consulting a legal professional can help you understand your legal requirements.

**27. letter**          If you apply for an ABN and you're not entitled, your application may be refused. If this happens, you'll be sent a letter clarifying why.

**28. iii**          Various information within Paragraph A.

**29. x**          Various information within Paragraph B.

30. **v**          Various information within Paragraph C.

31. **viii**        Various information within Paragraph D.

32. **i**           Various information within Paragraph E.

33. **vi**          Various information within Paragraph F.

34. **ii**          Various information within Paragraph G.

35. **(A) heat exchanger**     In solar thermal power plants, the heat from the sun hits a vast number of panels, which absorb the heat and transfer it to a liquid inside a tube that in turn goes to a heat exchanger.

36. **(A) turbine**       Inside the heat exchanger, the heat from the sun superheats water to create steam, which is used to spin a turbine and create the magnetic field that allows a generator to create electricity.

37. **electrical grid**    The electricity created is then sent to the electrical grid.

38. **FALSE**     Thanks to heat storage tanks, solar-thermal power plants in deserts can stock and supply electricity on demand twenty-four hours a day.

39. **NOT GIVEN**      There is nothing in the text relating to this and so the answer is 'not given' in the text.

40. **TRUE**     The technology is ready, but the main stumbling block that is preventing firms that are ready to put money into the projects is the lack of political and social stability in this region.

# EXAMPLE WRITING ANSWERS

Below you will find example writing answers for all the writing questions in the General Practice Tests 6 to 10. There are many ways of answering the writing questions and these examples are only one possibility of a good answer. Please refer to the question papers while you are reading these letters and essays so that you understand the questions that are being answered. We hope this will give you an insight into how the writing answers should be written for IELTS General module.

## GENERAL WRITING PRACTICE TEST 6

### Task 1

Dear Sir / Madam,

I have recently read about the evening course on the French language that your institution is offering and I have a few questions.

As I am an advanced speaker in French and have read that the Course "B1" is offered for this level, I would like to know what this course comprises, so that I will be able to decide whether this matches my abilities or whether I would need to sign up for another course. I would also like to know if the teachers giving the lessons are qualified native speakers, as I believe this is very important in order to get an authentic insight into the cultural context of the language studied. A native teacher has the greatest knowledge and understanding possible of the language he or she is teaching.

Lastly, I would like to ask for you to send me a brochure of the different courses offered at your institution, using the address I have sent this letter from as the recipient address.

I look forward to your response!

Yours sincerely,

Peter Travolta

*(180 words)*

**Task 2**

Regarding the question whether a country's government should be able to place a restriction on the number of children a family can have in order to control rising population numbers, I personally think that a government should not be able to take this step.

The concept of a government restricting the number of children a family can have was put into action in China as the one-child policy. Families were only allowed to have one child, which resulted in the deaths of many girls, as families thought boys were more useful in terms of supplying the family with money. If this restriction is imposed in western countries, I believe that the result will not be the same. However, in less economically developed countries, such as India or Kenya, the result would be the same as in China. In poorer countries, families require a large number of children, because for them children are a means of security. Due to poor hygiene conditions, many children die at young ages and therefore families need to have many children to ensure that at least one or two survive to become adults. Children are needed in poorer countries to supply the family with income and to furthermore care for parents once they are old. They are important economic factors and should therefore not be restricted. The proposed restriction would additionally breach people's human rights.

I believe that the government should not place a restriction on the number of children a family can have, but should ensure that all children have access to the same resources and have equal chances of achieving success. In poorer countries, children have to work and therefore do not have the opportunity to obtain a decent education, whilst in western countries children are educated and therefore have an advantage compared to children from poorer countries. By restricting the number of children a family can have, the opportunity disadvantage for children from poorer countries would increase even further, as they would have to work more and would obtain even less education.

In conclusion, the government should put more emphasis on creating equal opportunities for all children rather than limiting the number of children a family can have.

*(364 words)*

## GENERAL WRITING PRACTICE TEST 7

### Task 1

Dear Mr. Smith,

I have received your letter of complaint regarding poor service from a member of staff at my restaurant, The Seaside Inn.

I would like to use this opportunity to express my sincere apology for this embarrassing and rare occurrence at my restaurant. The member of staff responsible for your inconvenience has been removed from the list of waiters and is now working in the kitchen department, where contact with guests is unlikely. He has also undergone training to improve his attitude. The current staff have also undergone training again to avoid similar events in the future.

As a gesture of goodwill and as means of compensation, I would like to offer you a free meal for four people at my restaurant. You may use the enclosed voucher at any time and for any meal.

I hope to welcome you again as a guest at my restaurant!

Yours sincerely,

Katherine Hitchwell

Manager of The Seaside Inn

*(158 words)*

**Task 2**

Several schools around the world insist that all students should bring their own private laptop to class to assist in their education. Technology has become a significant component of educating children and is considered beneficial in many ways. Nonetheless, there are likewise many disadvantages to using private technological equipment in classrooms.

Bringing a private laptop to class offers a variety of benefits for students. Firstly, laptops can be used to take notes in classes where teachers sometimes speak at a high speed. Many children find that they can type faster than they can write by hand and therefore prefer typing their notes in class so as to not miss any important information. Teachers could furthermore make use of learning programs and websites during class, as students would have the possibility of using these websites on their private laptops. Moreover, students can use periods meant for working on assignments effectively, because they can work on their assignments digitally right away and not have to type up handmade notes later on. Information can additionally be distributed more easily to students, as for example hand-outs can simply be emailed or shared electronically and do not have to be printed.

Although bringing private laptops to class offers these various advantages, it also creates several disadvantages. Laptops firstly are fairly expensive, meaning that families with more than one child will have to spend a large amount of money to purchase laptops for all their children. Furthermore, laptops can easily be damaged during class and outside of class as well as stolen, which could create future costs for families. During class laptops can also distract students, because they can surf the Internet or look at non-class-related work during class periods. The amount of time students are exposed to technological equipment is also increased by incorporating laptops into classrooms, which can result in several health-related problems.

In conclusion, bringing a private laptop to class involves several advantages and disadvantages. Nonetheless, I personally believe that if used wisely, a laptop is an extremely useful tool in lessons and therefore I would support this initiative.

*(348 words)*

## GENERAL WRITING PRACTICE TEST 8

### Task 1

Dear Sir / Madam,

I am a regular customer at Nelly's supermarket and have never experienced a lack of quality in your products. However, last week, I made a rather disappointing purchase at your store that I would like to complain about.

Last Friday, I purchased a series of products that proved to be very unacceptable in quality and condition. Firstly, a bag of mandarins were completely covered in mould. I could not see this when I was at the supermarket, as the bag was covered in advertisements and the mandarins were not visible. Furthermore, I bought three pineapples, two of which had worms in the middle when I cut them open at home. Lastly, two sets of Vanilla Yoghurt were also three weeks past their sell-by date. This did not actually cause a problem as they were still in a good condition, but I noticed this as I began to inspect everything after having detected the damaged mandarins and pineapples.

I made these purchases on Friday the 12<sup>th</sup> of October, at around 3 p.m. in the afternoon and I would now like to know what you intend to do about this problem. Is there a possible refund or other means of compensation?

Regards,

John Bloomsrock

*(206 words)*

**Task 2**

Obesity has become a common problem in western societies and this is partly due to the availability of fast food at low prices. To tackle this problem, it has been suggested that governments should increase the tax on fast foods in order to reduce the amount of fast food consumed. I personally believe that this is a sound idea, because especially young people, who have less money, will be discouraged from buying fast food.

The main reason for the high consumption of fast food is that it is a cheap alternative to healthy meals. A salad for example often is twice as expensive as a burger, resulting in more people eating the burger than the salad. As a result, people prepare fewer meals themselves and eat more fast food instead. In my opinion, it should not be possible to sell fast food at a lower price than staple food. By making fast food more expensive than vegetables and fruit, people would change their eating habits, as they would want to save money.

Another way to reduce consumption of fast foods would be to prohibit its promotion. A similar approach was taken in terms of advertising cigarettes and one can say that this approach has been successful to some extent. Additionally, commercials for fast food often target young children through offering inducements, such as the toys in the happy meal at McDonalds for example. The children are persuaded to demand a happy meal, yet often do not necessarily want to eat the food contained in it. The only thing they want is the toy. If advertising fast food were forbidden, the number of children consuming fast food would be reduced and therefore the number of obese children would decrease as well.

In conclusion, governments should put a tax on fast food to reduce the amount consumed in order to decrease the number of obese people. By placing a tax on fast food and making it more expensive than healthy raw foods, people would began to eat more healthily. If additionally the advertising of fast food were banned, the number of obese people would decrease even more drastically.

*(356 words)*

## GENERAL WRITING PRACTICE TEST 9

### Task 1

Dear Tim,

I have decided to sell my car and I remember you being interested in it in the past. I am wondering whether you are still looking to buy a car and if this could be an offer that would interest you and suit your needs.

My car is now seven years old and therefore has a few drawbacks that you should be aware of. First of all, the radio is not adapted to modern standards. I know that you like to listen to electronic and bass music, so this may not satisfy you. Also, the seats are visibly damaged in the back, as my kids have sat there most of the time, but this is repairable.

Otherwise though, the car is in excellent condition and I am sure that, besides the radio, you will be pleased with its properties. It drives very well and will get you through the most stressful drive to work or an enjoyable holiday trip with success.

Just call me or write back if you would like to know more. I hope to see you soon if you would like to inspect and test drive my car!

Best wishes,

Thomas                                                                                  *(196 words)*

### Task 2

In many modern day families, it is a common aspect of family life that parents give jobs to their children to do around the house to develop their characters and a sense of self-sufficiency. This aspect can be looked at as having both positive and negative sides.

When parents give their children jobs or chores to do around the house, they make their children understand that they are part of a community. While this community is only within the family's house, the lessons children learn from carrying out their chores are equally fitting for the global community where they live in. Children are taught that they have to integrate into the global community and that in order for this community to work effectively, everyone must carry out their chores. Furthermore, children learn about the concept of pride, as they are taught to be proud of what they have accomplished. Chores around the house additionally prepare children for living independently later on in life, as they acquire skills that are valuable for everyday life.

Although there are many supporters of this concept, some parents argue that children should not be given jobs to do around the house. They argue that children should be allowed to be children and not have any duties. For them, children should be left as children and should not have to deal with any of the responsibilities adults have to deal with.

In conclusion, I believe that giving children chores to carry out is a positive aspect of family life, as I think that it helps children to become independent and makes it easier for them to live by themselves later on in life.                                                  *(277 words)*

## GENERAL WRITING PRACTICE TEST 10

**Task 1**

Dear Sir / Madam,

I recently requested a new credit card, as my old one was stolen during a holiday abroad. Even though the letter usually containing the credit card and its respective access information arrived on time, the credit card was missing and I would like to report this to you.

When the letter arrived, no visible signs were evident that the letter had been opened, but when I inspected the letterhead closely, there were small scratches that could indicate tampering. I believe that for security reasons this newly requested credit card should be cancelled immediately in order to avoid any criminal use. It may have been a technical issue, but it is also possible that a thief was responsible.

Lastly, I would like to know when a new credit card will be sent to me, as I will be going on a business trip in the near future and need it urgently.

Best wishes,

Marianne Bolton

*(158 words)*

**Task 2**

In modern day society, it has become common to make copyright protected material freely available on the Internet with the result that the owners of the work lose large sums of money. The discussion of whether or not this distribution is of positive or negative nature has therefore been raised. Personally, I believe that this issue has both negative and positive effects.

Distributing copyright protected material freely online can firstly help make this material more popular. Often people are not willing to spend money on a film or song before being exposed to it once, as they cannot be sure that they will enjoy the material they are about to purchase. If they purchase a song or film and then do not like it, the money spent will have been wasted, which is disappointing. Frequently, people purchase copyright protected material that they enjoyed after being exposed to it once, meaning that often owners often receive money at a later stage. An owner's reputation can additionally improve, because frequently owners who allow their work to be distributed partially or completely online have a more positive reputation amongst customers.

Regardless of the positive effects of the free online distribution of copyright protected material, it can be said that this distribution has several negative effects. Firstly, owners lose large sums of money through it. A lot of time and money can be spent producing the material distributed, as certain spaces and equipment must be rented or bought to produce a certain song or film. Like all other people, artists need money to survive and thus are at a disadvantage when they do not receive money for their work. I personally believe therefore that governments should make sure that when something is performed in public or when work is displayed in public, artists should receive credit and money.

In conclusion, it can be said that the online distribution of copyright protected material has both negative and positive effects. In my opinion, it cannot fully be determined whether this distribution is of a positive or negative nature; one must decide upon this for oneself.

*(349 words)*

# COMMENTARY ON THE EXAMPLE SPEAKING RECORDINGS

In this section you will find reports by an IELTS speaking examiner on the recordings of **Speaking Tests 6 - 10**. The questions asked in the recordings are the questions in the Speaking Tests 6 – 10, so, while listening to the recordings, it is advised to have the questions with you for reference. The recordings are not real IELTS test recordings, but the interviewer is a real IELTS examiner and the recordings are conducted in the exact way that an IELTS Speaking Test is done.

**SPEAKING PRACTICE TEST 6**

## Examiner's Commentary

The person interviewed is Roxanna, a Peruvian female. Roxanna is a teacher.

## Section 1

Roxanna spoke well and gave full answers. She was a little hesitant with her answer occasionally, but she communicated well. Her grammar was reasonably accurate, though there were errors and a limited range. Roxanna had a reasonable vocabulary range, though it tended to be a little basic. Roxanna's pronunciation was a little affected by her mother tongue, but this did not affect communication.

## Section 2

Roxanna gave a good and full section 2. She spoke reasonably slowly and with some hesitations, but her speech was perfectly coherent. Again, Roxanna's grammar and vocabulary range were a little limited. Her pronunciation was very clear and had the hint of a North American accent.

## Section 3

Section 3 was well dealt with by Roxanna, but the more demanding nature of the questions created her more problems. Roxanna attempted to answer every question, but some longer answers would have been better. Some basic errors came up ("childrens" instead of "children") and there was more hesitation in her speech.

**Marking** - The marking of the IELTS Speaking Test is done in 4 parts.

| | |
|---|---|
| Fluency and Coherence | 6 |
| Lexical Resource | 6 |
| Grammatical Range and Accuracy | 6 |
| Pronunciation | 7 |

**Estimated IELTS Speaking Band　　　6**

# SPEAKING PRACTICE TEST 7

## Examiner's Commentary

The person interviewed is Siva, an Indian male. Siva is a biochemist.

## Section 1

Siva spoke fluently and confidently and gave good and full answers. Siva's grammar was excellent and he used a wide range of structures flexibly and accurately. Siva's vocabulary was also excellent and he rarely paused to access language. Siva's accent was apparent, but did not interfere in any way with communication. Siva could also use English idiomatically and used humour appropriately.

## Section 2

Although Siva had an unsure start, he showed that he could speak at length with ease. His grammar usage and vocabulary were excellent again and he spoke clearly and fluently.

## Section 3

Siva's section 3 confirmed the impression he had made in the previous two sections. All aspects of his English were excellent and he spoke clearly, fluently and confidently. Again, he showed that he could speak idiomatically when appropriate.


**Marking** - The marking of the IELTS Speaking Test is done in 4 parts.

| | |
|---|---|
| Fluency and Coherence | 8 |
| Lexical Resource | 8 |
| Grammatical Range and Accuracy | 8 |
| Pronunciation | 8 |
| **Estimated IELTS Speaking Band** | **8** |

## SPEAKING PRACTICE TEST 8

### Examiner's Commentary

The person interviewed is Dimitry, a Georgian male. Dimitry is a student.

### Section 1

Dimitry spoke fluently, confidently and accurately. His Georgian accent was apparent, but it did not affect comprehension at all. He gave fairly full answers and showed that he had the ability to speak at length. Dimitry's vocabulary range was very wide and he also had a good idiomatic English usage. It was not perfect. Dimitry used the word "stressing" instead of "stressful," but incidents like this were not common. Dimitry's grammar usage was very accurate, but occasionally he made very minor errors, for example when he said "from 1920's" instead of the "from the 1920's," which reflects the different usage of articles in his mother tongue.

### Section 2

Dimitry showed in this section that he has no problem talking at length in English. Again, Dimitry used accurate grammar and a wide and idiomatic range of lexis. It was not perfect, with Dimitry choosing to use "advertisement" instead of the more natural "advertising," which is a common error in even strong English users.

### Section 3

Dimitry's performance in section 3 reflected his performances in the previous two sections and he showed this excellent use of English. The grammar and word choice were both accurate and varied. Again, he showed that he has an excellent idiomatic usage of English, mixing this with formal lexis use at the same time.

**Marking** - The marking of the IELTS Speaking Test is done in 4 parts.

| | |
|---|---|
| Fluency and Coherence | 9 |
| Lexical Resource | 8 |
| Grammatical Range and Accuracy | 8 |
| Pronunciation | 8 |

**Estimated IELTS Speaking Band**     **8**

# SPEAKING PRACTICE TEST 9

## Examiner's Commentary

The person interviewed is Katerina, a Czech female. Katerina works in business.

## Section 1

Katerina was a confident and fluent speaker. It was particularly noticeable that she was able to give long answers in accurate English to nearly all the questions asked. The interviewer therefore did not need to use all the questions in the test. Katerina also had a wide range of vocabulary and she did not need to pause to access lexis or grammar. There was the occasional awkward word choice (i.e. "far away from the centre" instead of "far from the centre"), but this did not affect communication. Katerina's accent was apparent and she made the occasional mispronunciation (i.e. "vineyards" and "picturesque"), but this did not affect comprehension in any way. Katerina's grammar was excellent with very few errors or awkward usage.

## Section 2

Katerina took the full minute to prepare, which is always advisable. She gave full answer when she started talking, with the interviewer having to stop her after two minutes, which shows the value to using the time. Again, Katerina's vocabulary, grammar and fluency were excellent. Her accent was again noticeable, but not intrusive in any way.

## Section 3

Katerina again performed well in section 3. She spoke fluently and accurately and again showed her wide range of vocabulary. She made the occasional errors (i.e. "the fast grow" instead of "the fast growth"), but these never affect communication or comprehension. Katerina's use of connectives and other cohesive features allow her to speak with great coherence. Overall, Katerina showed an excellent ability to deal with unexpected questions and subjects, being able to immediately come up with opinions in fluent English on all topics.

**Marking** - The marking of the IELTS Speaking Test is done in 4 parts.

| | |
|---|---|
| Fluency and Coherence | 8 |
| Lexical Resource | 8 |
| Grammatical Range and Accuracy | 8 |
| Pronunciation | 8 |
| **Estimated IELTS Speaking Band** | **8** |

## SPEAKING PRACTICE TEST 10

### Examiner's Commentary

The person interviewed is Toshe, a Japanese female. Toshe is a teaching assistant.

### Section 1

Toshe spoke well and generally quite fluently. Her English was strong, but there were certain limitations in her abilities and flexibility. She did not need to hesitate much to access vocabulary or grammar and her accuracy in both was very good, though not without error. Toshe's Japanese background is very apparent in her pronunciation, but this does not really affect her communicative ability.

### Section 2

Again, Toshe showed she had a good command of English with some limitations in her vocabulary and grammar usage. She spoke fairly fluently in this longer turn, and she only really hesitated from time to time in order to maintain the coherence of her speech rather than to access language.

### Section 3

Toshe again performed well in this section, though the more demanding nature of the questions brought out more hesitation and some errors. Although there was more hesitation, Toshe still managed to produce lengthy and intelligent answers to the questions. There was still some limited flexibility in structure and lexical usage. Toshe's accent still showed her Japanese mother tongue, but her pronunciation was nearly always fairly clear.

**Marking** - The marking of the IELTS Speaking Test is done in 4 parts.

| | |
|---|---|
| Fluency and Coherence | 7 |
| Lexical Resource | 7 |
| Grammatical Range and Accuracy | 7 |
| Pronunciation | 7 |

**Estimated IELTS Speaking Band**          **7**

# Listening Recordings' Transcripts

## LISTENING TEST 6 TRANSCRIPT

**This recording is copyright.**

**IELTS-Blog.com listening practice tests. Test six. In the IELTS test you hear some recordings and you have to answer questions on them. You have time to read the instructions and questions and check your work. All recordings are played only once. The test is in four sections. Now turn to section one.**

**Section one. You will hear a conversation between a man and a woman about a home insurance claim.**

**First you have some time to look at questions one to five.**

*(20 second gap)*

**You will see that there is an example. This time only, the conversation relating to this will be played first.**

| | |
|---|---|
| Milly | Good morning. |
| Graham | Good morning. How can I help you? |
| Milly | I don't know if you remember me. I bought my car and home insurance here eight months ago. |

**So, eight months is the correct answer.**

**Now the full test will begin. You should answer the questions as you listen, as the recording is not played twice. Listen carefully to the conversation and answer questions one to five.**

| | |
|---|---|
| Milly | Good morning. |
| Graham | Good morning. How can I help you? |
| Milly | I don't know if you remember me. I bought my car and home insurance here <u>eight months</u> ago. |
| Graham | Ah, yes. I remember your face, but not your name, I'm afraid. |
| Milly | Oh, that's OK. |
| Graham | So, what can I do for you? |
| Milly | I'm afraid we had a break-in at our house. I wasn't very sure how to start the process for the claim, so I thought I'd come back to you. I hope that's alright. |
| Graham | Of course. I'm so sorry you've had burglars. I'd be very happy to help. So, here's a claim form. You used Clover Insurance, didn't you? |
| Milly | That's right. |
| Graham | I'll need to take some details first. First of all, I need the names on your home insurance policy. |

Milly        It was my husband and I. My husband's name is Colin Hudson. That's Colin with one L, so it's <u>C - O - L - I - N</u>. Hudson is H - U - D - S - O - N. My first name is Milly, which is M - I - L - L - Y.

Graham        And what's your home address?

Milly        <u>Fifteen</u> Battersea Avenue, Endford. The postcode is EN six, nine GD.

Graham        Thank you. I'll just make a note of that. Do you have the home insurance policy document from Clover with you?

Woman        No. I'm afraid I left it at home. I meant to bring it, but with all that's been happening, it slipped my mind.

Graham        That's OK. Err, do you perhaps remember the policy number?

Milly        Actually yes. I've got it written down here in my diary that I carry. Err, it's <u>JU seven three one</u>.

Graham        Good. Let's see what the next thing is. Ah yes. There's a question about the type of policy you have with Clover. Do you know what kind of policy you signed up for? With Clover, it's usually basic, enhanced or premium.

Milly        It was the <u>premium policy</u>. Even the enhanced policy didn't give us the level of protection we required.

Graham        That's good for you now. The policy will cover everything that's missing.

Milly        I hope so!

Graham        Now, I suppose the police have visited you.

Milly        That's right.

Graham        Have they given you a case number?

Milly        Err, yes. They said that we'd need it for this process, so I wrote it down in my diary as well. It's quite long and all numbers. It's three one five, one six six, <u>four six two</u>.

Graham        OK, I've got all that.

**Before the conversation continues, you have some time to look at questions six to ten.**

*(20 second gap)*

**Now listen carefully and answer questions six to ten.**

Graham        Right, Mrs. Hudson. I need to take down some details of the burglary. Normally you'd do this on the form or you could do it online, but as I'm here, we can do it together.

Milly        Thanks very much.

Man        No problem at all. Now, of course the insurance company wants to know what things you want to claim for. This of course can be the things that were stolen, but, as you've got the top level insurance, any damage, such as windows broken or doors forced can be claimed for as well. You can also

Page 152

claim for any of the house keys and locks to be replaced, as thieves sometimes return to a house once they know they can break in more easily.

Milly            There was one window broken at the back, but the doors were all untouched. I don't think we need to worry about locks, as all the keys in the house were accounted for.

Graham        What burglars sometimes do is just take an impression for a key, so that people don't think to replace the locks.

Milly            Oh really! We'd better do that then. There were keys lying around.

Graham        Now, what else?

Milly            Some valuable things went missing.

Graham        Yes. That's usual.

Milly            My jewelry has all gone. I've made a list here for you.

Graham        Thanks.

Milly            Fortunately, my husband and I were both wearing our watches and my husband had his silver tie pin on the tie he was wearing. His silver picture frame with his family picture has gone, though. We also had quite a lot of cash in the house; around five hundred pounds, but we had it cleverly hidden, so they didn't find it.

Graham        Well done!

Milly            The only other thing gone is a painting. It was hanging on the wall above an antique table, which they didn't take. It was quite valuable, so the thieves must have been quite knowledgeable to recognise that. The table was more valuable and also had a valuable porcelain vase on it. The thieves didn't spot that either.

Graham        Is that all then?

Milly            Yes.

Graham        The final thing is to value everything.

Milly            I'm afraid that although I did that at home, I forgot that too. I can remember some things, though.

Graham        It doesn't matter. You can email me it all later.

**That is the end of section one. You will now have half a minute to check your answers.**

*(30 second gap)*

**Now turn to section two.**

**Section two. You will hear a man giving some people information about things to do in a seaside town. First you have some time to look at questions eleven to fifteen.**

*(20 second gap)*

**Now listen carefully to the information talk and answer questions eleven to fifteen.**

Hello everyone. It's a lovely morning today and we're apparently going to get lots of sun later. Now, here at the Seaview Hotel, we are very close to the beach and, given the weather, I thought I'd just let you know what you can do there.

If you leave the hotel from the back, take a left and follow the path down to the beach. You'll pass a mini-golf on the way on the right. It's not that expensive and if you've had enough of the beach, it's a really fun way to spend an hour.

When you get to the beach, you'll see the pier straight in front of you. It stretches out into the sea and is a nice walk out. It only costs a few dollars to walk on the pier, unless you want to go fishing, and then it costs a bit more.

On the left of the pier when you face the sea, there is of course the beach. You can lie down here and sunbathe. Swimming is very safe, but do check the large flags that the lifeguards put out. The lifeguards have their shed on the beach here just next to the pier. A green flag means that swimming is safe and this is usually what you'll see. Every now and then though, you'll see an orange flag. Then you shouldn't swim, usually because of a strong current. You'll see the flags at the back of the beach, just behind the lifeguard's shed and the paved path, which I'll tell you about now.

So, at the back of the beach, there is a large paved path. You can walk up and down this path at any time, as cars are not allowed here. Cyclists are allowed, but not between the hours of nine a.m. and six p.m.

A bit further down the beach on the left as you walk down the path, you can rent a chair to sit on if you don't like lying on a towel, mat or on the sand.

Now on the right of the pier as you face the sea is more beach, where you can lie down and relax. At the back of the beach and over the path just to the right of the pier, is a nice restaurant. It serves all sorts of things, from fish and chips to sandwiches and ice cream. They have a terrace on the roof where you can eat if the weather's nice or you can go inside if you've had enough sun or if the weather's bad.

Further down the beach on the right, you can rent a kayak. This is great fun and you can take one out for two hours and get away from the crowds. It's essential if you rent a kayak that you know how to swim and they will ask you that if you want to rent one. Also, they won't rent a kayak to anyone under the age of sixteen.

**You now have some time to look at questions sixteen to twenty.**

*(20 second gap)*

**Now listen to the rest of the information talk and answer questions sixteen to twenty.**

After you've had your nice day at the beach, you will have the evening to enjoy. If you fancy watching some live entertainment, there are two places you can go. Firstly, there is the Playhouse Theatre, which this evening is presenting Murder in the Library. This is a crime play that is sure to be a lot of fun. This begins at seven thirty and ends at ten. Secondly, if you'd prefer some music, there is the Summer Showhouse that tonight has a battle of the bands for young people. This starts a little earlier at seven and goes on until ten thirty. You'll be sure of getting a variety of different music from the young talent from the area. To find both of these places, go left out of the front of the hotel and walk down the road. You'll come to the Playhouse first. Then there's a garage and the Summer Showhouse is just after that. If you still fancy some more time on or near the beach, there is a firework display being held at ten o'clock at the end of the pier. You won't be allowed onto the pier at this time, so I think the best place to see it is on the beach with some friends! This can be very popular, so make sure you arrive in good time to get a good view. If there's no room, you can watch from the path or the areas behind the path.

Some people have asked me about food and there are plenty of restaurants and cafés all around the area near the hotel. A bonus for you is that there is a culinary festival this weekend. This takes place from around six in the town centre. There will be kiosks all around the square serving food and drinks from a variety of different cultures. Some of these will be fairly familiar, such as Chinese, Indian, French, Italian and Thai, but others will be less common. Examples will be Scandinavian, West African, Polynesian and Siberian, amongst others. This will all go on until around twelve.

Now, if it's raining, and there is a storm forecast, everything will still be going on, but don't forget an umbrella. However, if the rain puts you off, there's a cinema about five minutes walk away from the hotel. Just turn right when you leave the hotel. Another option is the Comedy Club, though this starts a little later and is a bit further away, needing a taxi rather than a walk or a bus to get there. Doors open at nine and it goes on until midnight. It costs ten dollars to go in.

**That is the end of section two. You will now have half a minute to check your answers.**

*(30 second gap)*

**Now turn to section three.**

**Section three. You will hear a student being interviewed at a university. First you have some time to look at questions twenty-one to twenty-five.**

*(20 second gap)*

**Now listen carefully and answer questions twenty-one to twenty-five.**

| Dr. Langer | So, thanks for coming in for this interview at our university, Richard. |
|---|---|
| Richard | Thanks for asking me, Doctor Langer. |
| Dr. Langer | So, I can see from your application form that you took a year off. |
| Richard | Yes, that's right. |
| Dr. Langer | Can you tell me about it? |

Richard        As you know, I did French and German at school, but I wanted to learn a language that was not from Europe before I started doing modern languages at university.

| Dr. Langer | Where did you go? |
|---|---|
| Richard | I decided to go to Cairo to learn Arabic. |
| Dr. Langer | Did you have any basic Arabic before you went? |
| Richard | I studied it myself a little bit, but it wasn't much to prepare for being in Cairo. |

Dr. Langer     Did you do a course?

Richard        Not straight away. I couldn't afford it. After getting somewhere to live, I got a job in a sports club. I'm a good tennis player and I gave lessons at a local tennis club in the mornings and afternoons.

Dr. Langer     Did you need a <u>work permit</u>?

Richard        Theoretically yes, but the tennis club wasn't worried about that. Later, when I saved some money, I took an Arabic course. My parents helped out with the costs of that as well.

Dr. Langer     Did you find Arabic difficult?

Richard        It depends. Initially it was hard, as it was so different, but I soon found out that the <u>grammar</u> was very straightforward. I found the pronunciation really difficult and the reading also was really hard. I had to master the alphabet, before I could start to make sense of it.

Dr. Langer     When did you start to become operational in Arabic?

Richard        In speaking, I could start having conversations after a couple of months. I had lots of opportunity at the tennis club to practice, but it was in the evenings when I would go to <u>cafés</u> and talk with people there that my spoken Arabic really took off. The locals were very friendly and delighted that I was trying to learn their language. Most people would chat to me.

Dr. Langer     And the reading and writing?

Richard        That took a lot longer and I'm still not great at it now. The good thing about the writing though is that all Arabic is the same when written, whereas the speaking versions can vary in dialects in all Arabic-speaking countries.

Dr. Langer     How did you like the food?

Richard        Cairo is a very cosmopolitan city and you can get all sorts of food there. The basic fare is rice, breads, grilled meats and salads. They also have lots of great dips to eat with vegetables and bread. I loved it. You had to learn where to go though, as the <u>quality</u> could be variable!

**You now have some time to look at questions twenty-six to thirty.**

*(20 second gap)*

**Now listen to the rest of the interview and answer questions twenty-six to thirty.**

Dr. Langer     I'm glad you seemed to enjoy your year in Cairo. So which two languages would you like to specialise in here?

Dr. Langer     That's a difficult question, as I'd like to continue with my French and German, but I don't want to abandon my Arabic. It would also be fun and useful to do another language from scratch. I'd be really keen to learn Chinese.

Dr. Langer     We don't offer that here I'm afraid, though we do the others.

Richard        I think I'll go for the <u>Arabic</u> and my best European language. My German is a bit rusty, but I also practised my French in Egypt. I'll go for the French, I think.

Page 156

Dr. Langer     That would be a good mixture.

Richard       Can I ask a couple of questions?

Dr. Langer     Of course.

Richard       I'd like first to know how the course is taught. I guess the usual university lecture style isn't suited to languages.

Dr. Langer     No, although when you study literature in your chosen languages, there are lectures. The first year of the course focuses on your getting a good knowledge of the grammar and vocabulary of your languages. This is done in kind of school-type lessons. Through the year, the key areas of grammar are covered. For developing your vocabulary, students will be assigned various readings on particular topics. These then will be discussed in smaller seminars.

Richard       How many people are in a seminar?

Dr. Langer     Usually six to ten. These sessions are led by a native speaker of your languages and the focus will be on developing fluency in speech and vocabulary.

Richard       That sounds good.

Dr. Langer     The second year continues with lessons to cover grammar, though usually more obscure or difficult points. The speaking seminars are replaced by seminars on literature and cultural topics. These seminars will be led by the same teachers as in the first year. There'll be lectures on literature as well.

Richard       And the third year?

Dr. Langer     You spend that in countries that speak the languages you are studying. You spend five months in each country.

Richard       What will I do in these countries?

Dr. Langer     You can either study or work. You have to study in a university that runs an approved programme or do a job that we agree to.

Richard       Can I get any help with these?

Dr. Langer     Yes. You can organise things yourself, but you have to make sure that the course you choose to study at the foreign university has to be an approved programme. If you can't find anything, we have a list of suitable universities in various countries and these universities are used to students coming from us. Jobs are probably harder to organise. You of course may have some friends overseas now who might be able to help. A lot of students have family who have business relationships in other countries and that can be a good way to find a suitable temporary job. If you want a job and can't find one, we have some contacts that we can use to place you.

Richard       And year four is back at the university, I suppose.

Dr. Langer     That's right. The grammar classes will be over then, but you'll have seminars discussing language points that you or your teachers bring up. Then there'll be more lectures on literature in the languages that you'll be studying.

Richard        I expect year four will have the final exams. Is that right?

Dr. Langer        Oh yes. You will have a series of exams. There will be an oral exam, which will be conducted by a native speaker teacher. That will be in early May. Then, at the start of June, the written exams will come. There will be two <u>translation</u> exams, a listening exam and two exams on literature. The literature exams will depend on which topics you choose. Your final course grade will be based on these exams combined with various assignments set over the course and a third year dissertation.

**That is the end of section three. You will now have half a minute to check your answers.**

*(30 second gap)*

**Now turn to section four.**

**Section four. You will hear part of an anthropology lecture on the match. First you have some time to look at questions thirty-one to forty.**

*(50 second gap)*

**Now listen carefully and answer questions thirty-one to forty.**

Good morning everyone and welcome to this lecture on anthropology. Today, we look at the phenomenon of fire and how the match was developed in our society. Fire was a basic need for modern humankind and a catalyst for the expansion of our ancestors beyond the borders of Africa. It gave us the power to survive in harsh environments, process food, and change the shape of the environment we live in.

As time passed, the ability to create fire became commonplace all around the world. However, that process was still slow, as fire is unreliable and dependent upon many conditions, such as rain and wind. Fire was also hard to <u>move</u>. Because of these problems, many scientists of the early human civilizations tried to find some way to make fire easy to create, portable and reliable. Because they lacked the knowledge of chemistry and physics, their early efforts were unsuccessful. The only relatively successful example of the early control over fire came from fifth century AD China, where sulfur coated wooden sticks were used as a catalyst to create fire. By the <u>tenth</u> century, manufacture of these fire inch-sticks could be found in all parts of China.

A thousand years passed, and scientists still did not come close to finding the way to create a self-igniting source of fire that could be used reliably by the general population. The basis of the modern match and lighter technology was founded in the second half of the seventeenth century by the alchemist Hennig Brandt, who dreamed of creating gold from other metals his entire life. During his career, he managed to extract pure phosphorus and test its <u>flammable properties</u>. His notes proved to be an important stepping stone for future generations of inventors.

The first match was created in eighteen oh five by Jean Chancel in Paris. This crude match looked nothing like the modern striking matches we use today. Instead of using phosphorus, Chancel coated wooden sticks with potassium chlorate, sulfur, sugar, rubber, and then dipped these sticks into a small asbestos bottle filled with sulfuric acid. Unfortunately, <u>nasty fumes</u> were released when the connection between the acid and the mixture on the stick was made to create fire. This could and did make many users of Chancel's match sick. The method was also a bit complicated, needing always a bottle of sulfuric acid at hand, and so did not achieve widespread popularity.

The next innovation in matches was introduced to the public in eighteen twenty-six by John Walker, an English chemist. He devised a way of igniting the match through using <u>friction</u>. The matches were made by combining a paste of sulfur with gum, potassium chlorate, sugar and ignited by drawing the match between a fold of sandpaper. Between eighteen twenty-seven and eighteen twenty-nine, Walker managed to develop his invention's use, but soon his invention lost popularity due to its <u>danger</u>. A flaming ball of material often separated from the rest of the match, falling to the floor and destroying carpets and dresses. Because of this, Walker's matches were quickly banned in France and Germany.

The next step was in the eighteen thirties, with the invention of the white phosphorus match by Frenchman Charles Sauria. This match worked well, but it had the disadvantage of <u>self-lighting</u> when no-one was around with the obvious results. By eighteen fifty, many countries banned production and sale of these dangerous objects.

Replacements for white phosphorus matches were safety matches that were developed by the Swede Johan Lundström in the late eighteen forties, although a different Swede had actually first patented this process. By utilising red phosphorus only on the <u>striking surface</u> and not on the match itself, the matches were made perfectly safe for the environment and health. By eighteen fifty-eight, Lundström had industrial manufacturing capabilities to create twelve million match boxes per year, and from that point on, their popularity rose until this match became the iconic object that is used today all around the world.

The problem of dangerous gas release was also solved by Lundström's safety match. The red phosphorus used does not release the same gases as white phosphorus. When the match is struck, the flame proceeds down the wooden stick, leaving only <u>harmless charcoal</u> behind, which is easily digestible by the environment when thrown away. When the flame is burning on the safety match, there are three phases of gas that are released. First and closest to the match is a hot pyrolysis gas. This is not dangerous to people, though of course it would burn the skin of anyone who came into contact with it. As the hot pyrolysis gas cools, it becomes a luminous yellow gas, which again would only be harmful because it is still relatively hot. Finally, as the luminous gas cools, the combustion products of the gases are released, which is seen as the <u>orange flame</u> that everyone recognises. These products dissipate into the air.

**That is the end of section four. You will now have half a minute to check your answers.**

*(30 second gap)*

**That is the end of listening test six. In the IELTS test you would now have ten minutes to transfer your answers to the listening answer sheet.**

## LISTENING TEST 7 TRANSCRIPT

**This recording is copyright.**

**IELTS-Blog.com listening practice tests. Test seven. In the IELTS test you hear some recordings and you have to answer questions on them. You have time to read the instructions and questions and check your work. All recordings are played only once. The test is in four sections. Now turn to section one.**

**Section one. You will hear a conversation between a man and a woman discussing a holiday the man recently came back from.**

**First you have some time to look at questions one to five.**

*(20 second gap)*

**You will see that there is an example. This time only, the conversation relating to this will be played first.**

| Vivienne | Hey Pete! Are you back from your holiday then? |
|---|---|
| Pete | Yes. I got back last night. |
| Vivienne | Where did you go? Wasn't it the US? |
| Pete | No. I went to Canada. |

**So, Canada is the correct answer.**

**Now the full test will begin. You should answer the questions as you listen, as the recording is not played twice. Listen carefully to the conversation and answer questions one to five.**

| Vivienne | Hey Pete! Are you back from your holiday then? |
|---|---|
| Pete | Yes. I got back last night. |
| Vivienne | Where did you go? Wasn't it the US? |
| Pete | No. <u>I went to Canada.</u> |
| Vivienne | So, tell me about it. |
| Pete | It started badly, as I missed my flight. |
| Vivienne | Oh no! What happened? |

Pete        <u>I got stuck in a traffic jam in my taxi.</u> Lots of cars were going to a different airport and the whole road was full of traffic.

| Vivienne | Oh no. That must have been terrible. Were you really stressed? |
|---|---|

Pete        I was at first. When I realised that there was no way to get to the flight though, I felt better, as there was nothing else to do but wait until I spoke to someone at the airport.

Vivienne        Did you have to pay for another flight?

Pete        Fortunately not. I could have gone the same day on a later flight, but I would have had to pay for that. I got one the next day without having to pay.

Vivienne        Well, at least that was something. You missed a whole day of holiday though.

Pete        Yes. It was a bit annoying, but I had only myself to blame. I know the roads can be bad. I should have stayed nearby to the airport the night before.

Vivienne        Did the airline put you up in a hotel?

Pete        It wasn't their fault that I missed the flight, so no. They did give me a food voucher though, as I had to hang around for a long time. In the end, I stayed with my old friend Mike. He doesn't live too far from the airport. I had to get a taxi there though and back again the next morning and that wasn't cheap.

Vivienne        How was the flight itself?

Pete        I was flying to Toronto and it took around seven and a half hours. Unfortunately, I had left my book in my main check-in baggage, so the time passed slowly.

Vivienne        Why didn't you watch a movie?

Pete        That makes me sick on a plane. It's hard for me to drop off to sleep as well, as my neck gets stiff. It was good that I had two interesting people who sat next to me, so we had a conversation about Canada off and on for the whole flight. I learned quite a few things that I didn't know.

Vivienne        I hope all the disasters were over by the time you reached Canada!

Pete        Almost. It was quick to get through immigration, but then I found after a very long wait that there had been a mix up back in England with my missed flight. My bags never made it on the plane and no-one knew where they were. I had to spend twenty-four hours in Toronto with only the clothes I'd travelled in.

Vivienne        You're lucky it wasn't winter!

Pete        Absolutely. I'd have frozen to death without winter clothing! Anyway, that was the last disaster! The rest of the holiday was great!

**Before the conversation continues, you have some time to look at questions six to ten.**

*(20 second gap)*

**Now listen carefully and answer questions six to ten.**

Vivienne        How was Toronto?

Pete        It was great! There was so much to see and do there. I needed more time really, as I was only there for three days. I needed a week.

Vivienne        What sort of things did you do then?

Pete            I wanted to orientate myself to begin with, so I decided to go to the CN Tower and look around. Unfortunately, the lifts were closed for a week because of maintenance, so I had to give that a miss.

Vivienne        That was a shame.

Pete            Yes. Instead, the first morning, I visited Fort York in the western downtown area. You know I have an interest in military history. There was an exhibition on there about nineteenth century military uniforms. It was great.

Vivienne        I can imagine that you would've liked that. Did you manage to visit the Royal Ontario Museum? I told you about that before you left.

Pete            I checked out their website and it just wasn't something that I felt would interest me. I appreciate you telling me about it, though. While I was researching it, I found out about the Air and Space Museum and I saw that on the second morning.

Vivienne        How about the Art Gallery of Toronto?

Pete            Again, I didn't think that would be of interest to me, but you know, I decided I should be a bit more open, so I gave it a go. It wasn't the most exciting experience in the world for me, but in the end I was glad I tried it out.

Vivienne        Did you get to see any sporting action when you were there? I know you're a big sports fan.

Pete            I wanted to go to a hockey game and I went to the stadium, but it was out of season. The Hockey Hall of Fame made up for it though. I spent nearly five hours there looking around.

Vivienne        It's a shame about the game, though.

Pete            Yes, but I did get to see the Bluejays play at the Rogers Centre.

Vivienne        Is that football?

Pete            No. They have football matches at the Rogers Centre, but this was baseball.

Vivienne        Did you understand the rules?

Pete            I think so. It was a bit complicated, but I found it easier than football. There was also a guy sitting next to me who explained. He was a real basketball fan, but he knew his baseball too.

Vivienne        It sounds like you were pretty busy.

Pete            Yes, and that was just the first two days.

**That is the end of section one. You will now have half a minute to check your answers.**

*(30 second gap)*

**Now turn to section two.**

**Section two. You will hear a man giving some people information about a farm visit. First you have some time to look at questions eleven to fifteen.**

*(20 second gap)*

**Now listen carefully to the information talk and answer questions eleven to fifteen.**

Hello, everyone. Today you've come to the Open Day at Sunnyside Farm. To start with, I'd like to tell you a little about our history and what we do here.

The Wilson family have been farming here at Sunnyside since the start of the last century. To start with, it was mainly an arable farm, which means that there were no animals. To start with, Sunnyside specialised in growing <u>vegetables</u>. The produce would then be sold in local markets around the area. At that time, the farm became a major source of work for the local population, especially in summer time and the harvest period.

After the First World War, the farm turned towards meat production. The farm had a herd of cows for producing beef and also several hundred sheep to produce lamb every spring. Rather uncommon for a British farm, the meat produced was sold for <u>export</u>. This carried on for around fifty years, with the interruption of course of the Second World War. At the time of the war, the farm actually closed down for while, as most labourers and the farmer himself were away in the army. The farm started up again when peace returned. In the early seventies, the farmer at that time saw that he would earn better margins producing milk. He bought a herd of dairy cattle and sold the other animals. This was a major change and quite a big commercial risk, as the farmer also had to equip his dairy to get the milk from the cows and this was quite expensive. However, the gamble paid off and Sunnyside became a successful producer of milk for the whole area.

Around ten years ago, milk became less and less profitable. This was because some big companies created increased <u>competition</u> after they bought up some of the surrounding farms and started producing cheap milk. The farmers at Sunnyside at that time are the same ones as today, Mr. and Mrs. Wilson. They had been interested in farm tourism for some time, as they had seen it work quite well up in Scotland, where they had gone on a <u>holiday</u>. They saw how popular this was and, after some research, they saw that no-one else in the area was doing anything like this. After a year of planning, they took the plunge and bought a wide variety of different farm animals that people could come and see and interact with. Naturally, this project is predominantly targeted at <u>children</u>, though you'd be surprised how many adults come by themselves for the experience.

**You now have some time to look at questions sixteen to twenty.**

*(20 second gap)*

**Now listen to the rest of the information talk and answer questions sixteen to twenty.**

So, let me now tell you about some of the things that we do here. We have a number of different animals for people to interact with and other things to do as well. To start with, people can visit <u>the Old Dairy, which is where the cows used to be milked. Here, there is a small museum on dairy farming.</u> A short film is played here every half an hour. <u>If you actually want to try milking some cows yourself, go to the West Stable.</u> This takes place twice a day, at nine thirty a.m. and four-thirty p.m.

Another area of farming that we cover is the lamb industry. <u>In the East Barn, you can see the sheep close up and in season you can see and feed the lambs.</u> There is also an exhibition on the history of the sheepdog, which of course has always been a vital companion of the sheep farmer. Every afternoon at two p.m., <u>you can see an exhibition of sheepdog skills in the South Field.</u> This goes on for around twenty-five minutes.

In the North Field, we have a favourite for all ages. There you can find our donkeys and horses. These can be fed or ridden on. It's important to have adults with children if they want to try the riding out. If the children are very young or nervous, it's best to try a donkey. All our donkeys are very placid and good-natured. In three months, the horses and donkeys will move to the West Field, as <u>we are planning a camp site in the North Field.</u> People will be then able to stay overnight at the farm in tents or caravans. I've mentioned quite a few locations so far. Don't worry! Just outside this building is a map of all the activities and where to find them. Any questions so far?

**That is the end of section two. You will now have half a minute to check your answers.**

*(30 second gap)*

**Now turn to section three.**

**Section three. You will hear a man and a woman discussing some work training. First you have some time to look at questions twenty-one to twenty-five.**

*(20 second gap)*

**Now listen carefully and answer questions twenty-one to twenty-five.**

| | |
|---|---|
| Grace | Hello, Dominic. Can I have a word? |
| Dominic | Oh, hello, Grace. Of course you can. |
| Grace using. | You know you applied for that extra training on the new computer software that we're |
| Dominic | Yes. |
| Grace | Well, I managed to push it through. |
| Dominic | That's great. I thought it would be rejected, because it was too expensive. |
| Grace | There were certainly objections raised to that, but <u>the main problem was that they didn't want you away on the days of the training. You'll be away in San Francisco while we're having the big sales meeting.</u> |
| Dominic | So what happened? |
| Grace | I said I'd be able to fill in for you if you told me the key things needed for the customers. |
| Dominic | Thanks so much, Grace. |
| Grace | When can we meet so that you can fill me in then? |

Page 164

Dominic        How about just before the normal start of work on Monday? We can arrive an hour early and I'll have everything ready?

Grace        I drive my daughter to school on Mondays, so it's hard for me to get here that early. How about at the end of the working day on Friday?

Dominic        I'm leaving here at lunchtime that day, as I have a meeting in town about the new parts we're ordering. The only time I'm really free is Thursday morning.

Grace        I'm in a meeting that time. Hmm. Look. I'll ask my friend Angie to take my daughter into school on Monday. That way we can meet as you first suggested.

Dominic        Good. Thanks, Grace. You'll need to have your computer with you, so that I can upload some stuff.

Grace        Will there be a lot to do?

Dominic        Not really. I can explain all the rationale behind the design decisions to you and if you make some brief notes, that'll be enough. I'll also explain the model that we've made to show the customers. It'll be quite straightforward, as it's similar to the last one we did for the previous contract. The model is in my office. Finally, I'll also upload the sales forecasts to you, as you'll need that to prove that our ideas are right.

Grace        Good. That's all clear. Now do you have any questions about the training? I've just read up about it for you.

Dominic        Oh good. Well, first of all, I'll need to stay overnight in San Francisco. How shall I pay for everything? I paid in advance myself last time and then got the money back from the company.

Grace        That's always a bit of a pain, though. You have to collect and keep all the receipts safe. I know the company card is not being used, so I'll make sure you get that.

Dominic        That's good. I don't like having to pay these expensive hotels myself as my credit card is nearly always maxed out. The company is not keen on giving out cash in advance either!

Grace        No. That's not popular here!

Dominic        The next thing is how the company would like me to travel to the training. The bus is the cheapest, but I'd like to work on my computer and that's not very easy on a bus.

Grace        No, it isn't! It's also not really far enough for a plane journey either. Is there a train?

Dominic        Yes. Amtrak has a service there.

Grace        What would you prefer?

Dominic        Anything but the bus really. I'd even drive rather than take the bus and miss the work on the journey.

Grace        I'll make a train booking for you. Driving will be too tiring for you and you want to arrive fresh and alert.

Dominic     OK. Thanks.

**You now have some time to look at questions twenty-six to thirty.**

*(20 second gap)*

**Now listen to the rest of the discussion and answer questions twenty-six to thirty.**

Grace     Now, I want to explain where your training is. It's at the Green Bay Business Park. You know where that is?

Dominic     Yeah. I've been there before.

Grace     Do you know the Forward Thinking Training Center as well?

Dominic     No. I've never been to that training company before.

Grace     OK. So, you arrive at the main gates. Go in and take the middle road. That will take you past the mobile phone company on the right and the GPS Center on the left.

Dominic     Just a moment, Grace. I'll just get some paper. I'll need to write it down or I'll forget.

Grace     No problem.

Dominic     OK. Here we are. I'm just making a note of what you just said. Right, carry on.

Grace     So, after you pass the mobile phone company and the GPS Center, take the next right and then first left. Go a hundred metres down that road and Forward Thinking will be on the left, with a radio station opposite.

Dominic     That seems fairly straightforward. You know, I think I do know this actually. I went there last year for an accountancy training.

Grace     That's right. I went on that for a different account there as well.

Dominic     Yes. It was a good training. So, I know where it is now. When you pass Forward Thinking, then there's a dead end with a recycling depot.

Grace     Yes, that's right. You've got it.

Dominic     Now, do I need to take anything with me? My company ID for instance?

Grace     Let's have a look at this letter. No ID is required. It says you only need to bring this confirmation letter. You can take your computer for making any notes you like.

Dominic     OK. That'll be useful.

Grace     Yes. It says here too that lunch will be provided and drinks throughout the day. They'll also give you a password to get online there, so you can keep in touch with us if necessary.

**That is the end of section three. You will now have half a minute to check your answers.**

*(30 second gap)*

**Now turn to section four.**

**Section four. You will hear a presentation on obesity and sugary drinks. First you have some time to look at questions thirty-one to forty.**

*(50 second gap)*

**Now listen carefully and answer questions thirty-one to forty.**

Good afternoon everyone and thanks for coming to my presentation today, which is on the link between childhood obesity and sugary drinks.

Childhood obesity is a worrying phenomenon that affects many developed societies. Childhood obesity rates have doubled throughout the past thirty years in the United States for children aged two to five and twelve to nineteen, and tripled in the age group of six to eleven.

Many social and environmental pressures lead to greater obesity in children. Chief among these influences is the wide variety and availability of sugar-sweetened drinks that contain little to no nutritional value. These beverages include soft drinks, sports drinks, fruit drinks, flavored teas and coffees and energy drinks. Throughout the past ten to fifteen years, these drinks have exploded on to the consumer scene, flooding grocery stores, gas stations, convenience stores and vending machines.

Americans have doubled their consumption of soda pop in the last twenty-five years, a trend that closely follows the obesity epidemic. The average American drinks one point six cans of soda pop a day, which is more than five hundred cans a year. Soda drinking is particularly rampant among teenagers. Data indicates that soft drinks account for thirteen per cent of a teenager's caloric intake, by far the largest source of calories in his or her diet. For decades, milk was the most common beverage consumed by children, but by the mid nineteen nineties, boys and girls were drinking twice as much soda pop as milk.

One recent study has demonstrated a strong link between consumption of sugar-sweetened beverages and childhood obesity. Although some studies conflict regarding the causality between sugar-sweetened beverages and obesity, a number of research studies confirm the findings that increased soft drink and sugar-laden beverage consumption is a risk factor for obesity. Not only do sugar-sweetened drinks likely lead to obesity, they are also associated with tooth decay and fragile bones.

Energy and soft drinks can also contain large amounts of caffeine. The amounts of caffeine found in such drinks are often about ten grams per ounce. With that in mind, take a look at the amount of caffeine found in other beverages. Most experts recommend that children consume well under a hundred grams of caffeine per day. The pharmacological effects of caffeine are notable in children, most commonly seen as hyperactivity, sleep disturbances and restlessness. Drinking large amounts of caffeine can also be associated with high blood pressure and frequent headaches.

Researchers have reported that a new practice among college-age students is the simultaneous consumption of energy drinks and alcohol, which allows greater consumption of alcohol since alertness is perpetuated by the energy drink. In addition, the sugar content of energy drinks is comparable or higher than most soft drinks with, for example, a typical energy drink containing twenty-seven grams of sugar. Alcohol usually contains a lot of sugar and this can lead to massive sugar intakes for people who mix energy drinks with alcohol.

So what can be done to limit the amount of the nutritionally-poor liquid calories that children and adolescents are consuming? On an individual basis, the best approach is simply to replace soda and sports drinks with water or <u>low-fat milk</u> in children's diets. Water is the best hydrator available. Low-fat milk not only hydrates, but delivers calcium, protein and vitamin D.

What happens at school may be out of the immediate control of a parent, but parents can petition the school to eliminate <u>machines</u> that sell soft drinks and energy drinks in favor of bottled water. Children should be watched at home regarding their choice of liquids. A glass of a hundred per cent fruit juice per day is fine, but excessive soda, sports drinks or energy drinks is unhealthy. Parents need to provide guidance to their children, so that they know and understand this.

<u>Moderation</u> in guiding children, of course, is appropriate. Children who are constantly deprived of treats are more likely to binge eat or drink. Studies suggest that children who are raised by parents who exert excessive dietary restraint may be more likely to become obese.

Also, the <u>role models</u> presented by parents are important. Children possess the ability to regulate their caloric intake. However, if they see their parents struggle with the effort to control food or drink intake and the conscious restriction of intake to control weight, they may pattern their own eating and drinking behaviour after their parents instead of allowing their internal energy regulation to guide them. This in turn seems to lead to greater obesity in children.

In conclusion, parents should adopt healthy eating and drinking patterns, limiting the consumption of soft drinks and other sugar-sweetened drinks, and to do so without obsession. Helping children develop a love for the refreshing taste of water or a cold glass of milk will pay immediate health rewards for children as well as dividends for their future health and weight control. <u>Careful education</u> of today's youth will be the key to them avoiding these destructive drinks.

**That is the end of section four. You will now have half a minute to check your answers.**

*(30 second gap)*

**That is the end of listening test seven. In the IELTS test you would now have ten minutes to transfer your answers to the listening answer sheet.**

## LISTENING TEST 8 TRANSCRIPT

**This recording is copyright.**

**IELTS Blog.com listening practice tests. Test eight. In the IELTS test you hear some recordings and you have to answer questions on them. You have time to read the instructions and questions and check your work. All recordings are played only once. The test is in four sections. Now turn to section one.**

**Section one. You will hear a conversation between a man and a woman as they discuss a holiday.**

**First you have some time to look at questions one to five.**

*(20 second gap)*

**You will see that there is an example. This time only, the conversation relating to this will be played first.**

Keith          Good morning. My name is Keith Waters. I'm interested in finding out about a certain type of holiday. Would you be able to help me with that?

Penny          Welcome to Sunshine Tours agency. My name's Penny. Yes, I'm sure I can help you with that. What exactly are you thinking about?

Keith          My wife and I are interested in a cruise of the Mediterranean.

**So, cruise is the correct answer.**

**Now the full test will begin. You should answer the questions as you listen, as the recording is not played twice. Listen carefully to the conversation and answer questions one to five.**

Keith          Good morning. My name is Keith Waters. I'm interested in finding out about a certain type of holiday. Would you be able to help me with that?

Penny          Welcome to Sunshine Tours agency. My name's Penny. Yes, I'm sure I can help you with that. What exactly are you thinking about?

Keith          My wife and I are interested in a <u>cruise</u> of the Mediterranean.

Penny          That's a nice idea! A cruise on a ship in the Mediterranean is very popular right now. Can I take some basic details from you first, so I can work out what kind of cruise might suit you?

Keith          Of course.

Penny          So, your name is Keith Waters. And your wife's?

Keith          Her name is Melissa Waters.

Penny          Would you spell Melissa for me?

Page 169

| Keith | It's M - E - L - I - S - S - A. |
|---|---|

Penny       And it's just you and your wife?

Keith       That's right. We don't have any children.

Penny       OK. Let me make a note of that. Fine. Now, how old are you both?

Keith       I'm thirty-two and my wife's thirty.

Penny       Thank you. Now, I'd like to ask about your interests and hobbies. This will help in choosing the right cruise for you.

Keith       We're both keen on travelling, of course. That's why we'd like to go on a cruise. We're also quite sporty. We both swim and jog quite a lot. We're interested in cinema and history. Melissa is also a keen fiction reader, but I prefer non-fiction.

Penny       What kind of budget were you thinking about?

Keith       We can spend between seven thousand and eleven thousand dollars on the trip. As cheap as possible of course is best!

Penny       Right. I've got all that down. Now, I need to know when you'd like to go on your cruise and for how long?

Keith       Our holiday window starts on the first of July and ends on the sixteenth of July.

Penny       OK.

Keith       And as for length, we'd like to have at least fourteen nights on the ship.

Penny       Thank you. I'm sure that'll be possible.

**Before the conversation continues, you have some time to look at questions six to ten.**

*(20 second gap)*

**Now listen carefully and answer questions six to ten.**

Penny       Right. I've got all that down and I've got some ideas for you.

Keith       I'll just make some notes while I listen, if that's alright?

Penny       Of course. So, we have two boats that fit the dates you want. They sail on different dates, so that gives you some flexibility. First of all, I'd like to suggest the cruise on the boat the Maria Cristina. It's a Spanish boat and you'd fly to Barcelona to join her. The cruise from there costs ten thousand five hundred dollars for both of you, although the flights to get to Barcelona will be extra. With that, you have all food and drinks free during the voyage. You get an inside cabin, which means that you don't get a sea view, but you can upgrade to a sea view for a further eight hundred dollars. They have a cinema on board with different films every night and there are also lectures on the places where you will be visiting. There are also classes that you can do, for example, painting, cooking, art appreciation and others.

Keith          That's just in our budget, but an upgrade would put us over.

Penny          Yes, you'd have to do without the upgrade. <u>Travel insurance</u> is incorporated within the price though.

Keith          What about the next one?

Penny          That's the Sea Queen. This is also a Spanish boat, but it sails from Marseille in France and follows the same route as the Maria Cristina. Barcelona is the last stop before arriving back in Marseille. This costs <u>nine thousand</u> dollars for both of you, but this includes the return flights to Marseille. With this package, you do get a sea view and food is inclusive throughout the voyage. All drinks excluding water are extra though. There are fewer things going on. There is a cinema, but there are no lectures or classes. There is a <u>swimming pool</u> and gym though, so you'll be able to keep up with your exercise.

Keith          That's quite a lot of information, so I'd better get back and speak to my wife. She can come back here with me in two days, so I'll expect we'll have chosen which boat to go on by then. We can talk further details when we come in then.

Penny          That's great. See you in two days.

Keith          Yes. See you soon.

**That is the end of section one. You will now have half a minute to check your answers.**

*(30 second gap)*

**Now turn to section two.**

**Section two. You will hear a man and a woman on a radio programme, as the man gives an information talk on a reading charity. First you have some time to look at questions eleven to fifteen.**

*(20 second gap)*

**Now listen carefully to the information talk and answer questions eleven to fifteen.**

Marianne       Good morning everyone and welcome to Radio Star, your local radio station. Today we are joined by Jake Matthews, who is part of the Read for All charity. He has come in today to tell us a little about it. Welcome, Jake.

Jake           Thanks, Marianne.

Marianne       So, tell us all about Read for All, Jake.

Jake           Well, as the name implies, we are a charity that is focused on ensuring that all children have access to appropriate reading books. It has long been acknowledged that reading is an essential part of education while growing up and children who read a lot do better at school than their peers who do not read a lot. Our plan starts when children are very young, so of course, we therefore need to aim at parents, and chiefly <u>low income</u> patients, to educate them about the benefits to their children if they are

Page 171

read to. Many children who read a lot develop this love of reading when their parents read to them. If we can get this happening, then more children will grow up with an attachment to reading that will affect them positively for the rest of their lives.

Marianne     How do you educate the parents?

Jake          Our key focus is at <u>hospitals</u>, where children are born. We have plenty of leaflets about us and we have volunteers who visit the areas where parents are in hospitals and distribute these leaflets. Other places where we distribute our leaflets are nurseries, kindergartens and primary schools when parents drop off or pick up their children. The parents can then read about the benefits of reading in our leaflets and also see how we can help.

Marianne     How can you help?

Jake          Good question. We realise that one of the things that stops parents reading to their children is that they do not know which books to read or where to find them. Families on budgets also find it difficult to allocate money to this area of family life when things are so tight. Getting parents to think about these things is also hard if the parents are not readers themselves. If we can get parents to come to our centre or <u>website</u>, we can tell them how to find books at no cost through joining libraries or they can take away free books that we manage to print at a very low cost. All our books are graded by age and there are no issues with breaking copyright, as we have permission to use all of them. Also, we have a low cost app that people can download to their smart phone, as it seems even low budget families can afford to own smart phones! It only costs <u>a dollar</u> and with the app, stories and books can be downloaded for free and the stories can either be read by the parent or read by a recorded voice. Of course, we try and encourage the parents to do the reading, because of all the added benefits that this brings. This has already been a huge success and we believe that there are now thousands more parents reading to their children than when we started. This will make such a difference to the children's imagination and English skills. Linked to this, <u>immigrant</u> families can read or listen to the stories and both the parents and children's' English can be improved.

**You now have some time to look at questions sixteen to twenty.**

*(20 second gap)*

**Now listen to the rest of the information talk and answer questions sixteen to twenty.**

Marianne     How do you fund all these activities?

Jake          We only manage to operate because of generous donations. We get no official help. <u>We have one particular donor, who supplies the funding for at least sixty per cent of our needs</u>, but the rest all comes from the public. We have various ways that we try to raise funds. We run car boot sales, special dinners and other similar activities. We also ask people who use our products a lot to make a modest and optional donation, if they can afford it.

Marianne     Do you get enough money each year then?

Jake          Not always. Sometimes we make a little more than we need and sometimes a little less, but at present it all evens out in the end. We'd do better with more money though.

Marianne      I'm sure many of our listeners would be keen to help out. How can they find out how to get money to you?

Jake        Thanks very much for the suggestion. <u>We have a website called readforall.com. There is an icon on the home page labelled "Donations". If any of your listeners click on that, they will see the process of how to make a donation.</u> This will probably be more convenient than sending money by mail or trying to find one of our centres. Thanks very much to anyone who does this!

Marianne      I'm sure you'll get a good response.

Jake        I'd like to tell you now a little about volunteering, as we've received some questions about that.

Marianne      Of course.

Jake        We cannot afford to pay a salary to anyone who comes to do any work for us, although <u>sometimes we can pay for some modest expenditure incurred for travel from where people live to our centres if we can get receipts.</u> This will all be explained in our volunteer leaflets that can be picked up at our centres or found on the website, but I just wanted to make this clear up front. Now I'd like to let people know about where to come if they'd like to volunteer. The best place is to come to our town centre offices. To get there, you need to travel to the city centre and go down Ballard Street, which comes off the roundabout in the town centre. <u>Go down Ballard Street and take the second right. You'll recognise the turning, as there's a cinema on the corner. Across Ballard Street from it, there is a police station. So, you go down the road on this turning for around a hundred metres. On the left are our offices, above a car dealership. It's pretty easy to find us. If you come by car, you can park on the street and there are of course lots of buses that go to the town centre. If you can't find us, give us a call or ask for directions to the main town post office, which is right opposite our offices.</u>

**That is the end of section two. You will now have half a minute to check your answers.**

*(30 second gap)*

**Now turn to section three.**

**Section three. You will hear a university teacher and three of his students discussing the students' upcoming economics essays. First you have some time to look at questions twenty-one to twenty-five.**

*(20 second gap)*

**Now listen carefully and answer questions twenty-one to twenty-five.**

Amy        Good morning, Mr. Stevenson.

Mr. Stevenson      Good morning, Amy. Are William and Anna with you?

Amy        They're just coming. Here they are.

Mr. Stevenson        So, good morning. Now we're all here, let's begin. You've all got your extended economics essays due in next month and so we're meeting here today to discuss your progress. So, Amy. Tell me a little about your essay.

Amy              It's going fine, Mr. Stevenson. I chose to examine how global <u>oil prices</u> have affected the car industry.

Mr. Stevenson        That's a good subject at the moment. Those price fluctuations are creating some very unexpected results. Have you had any problems with gathering enough information to shape your essay?

Amy              Oh yes. As you said, it's very topical at the moment and everyone seems to be writing about it. I've more than enough information. Actually, my main headache is with my sources. I don't have much experience with an essay of this type and I'm not used to creating the <u>citations</u> in the correct way.

Mr. Stevenson        Yes. The first time that people write an essay at this level they often have problems with sources. Once you've done a few essays here, you'll learn what to do and you won't have any further problems. We try to help students with this area on our website, where we have a <u>guidance sheet</u> that details all the procedures that you'll need.

Amy              Oh good. I'll check that out.

Mr. Stevenson        Now, how about you, William? You're writing about the Australian fishing industry, aren't you?

William        Things are pretty good, thanks, Mr. Stevenson. I'm not writing about the fishing industry any more though. That was my original choice, but I found that the sources weren't very good for that.

Mr. Stevenson        Really! I thought lots would've been written about that.

William        Well, yes, a lot has been written, but not an awful lot recently. Because there was a shortage in fish stocks around ten years ago, most writers have focused on that, which means that today's normal situation doesn't attract much attention. Because of that, I decided to write about the effects of <u>immigration</u> on employment figures in the Northern Territory state in Australia.

Mr. Stevenson        And things are going fine, you say?

William        Yes, I've got plenty of up-to-date sources, but I have a problem with length. I seem to have gone about two thousand words over the four thousand word limit. I've reviewed my content and everything I've written is relevant and there's nothing to cut.

Mr. Stevenson        Writing too much is a common problem with essays as well. What I can suggest is that you work on the task of <u>revision</u>. Most people find that they are very wordy in their first drafts and things can be expressed in a much better way with fewer words. I've no doubt that you'll be no different. It will be quite time-consuming, but go through your work sentence by sentence. You'll soon find the length of your essay will soon be acceptable.

**You now have some time to look at questions twenty-six to thirty.**

Page 174

*(20 second gap)*

**Now listen to the rest of the discussion and answer questions twenty-six to thirty.**

Mr. Stevenson        That just leaves you, Anna. How's your essay going?

Anna        Not so well, I'm afraid, Mr. Stevenson. I've had lots of problems getting started because other essays were due for other teachers. <u>When I was finally ready to start your essay at the beginning of this month, I got ill and I spent quite a few days in bed.</u> I even went home to my parents' house, so I could recover properly.

Mr. Stevenson        Oh dear. That's quite serious. Do you think you'll be able to submit the essay by the deadline?

Anna        I don't know. I'm finding it hard to settle down and put in the amount of work needed to do a good job. I find the library distracting, because of all the people coming and going and my house mates are too noisy to allow me to concentrate when I'm at home.

Mr. Stevenson        <u>Maybe you could come to my special evening work sessions. It's just a quiet time when students who find it hard to work independently at home or in the library can work without being disturbed. I'll be there as well, so if you have any questions, you'll have no delay in getting an answer.</u>

Anna        That's a good idea, Mr. Stevenson, but what I really need is an extension, so that I can really do a really good job on the essay.

Mr. Stevenson        That shouldn't be a problem, Anna, but we have to follow the department rules on that. <u>They specify that you need to supply a doctor's note for what you're asking for. If you can do that, then I will fill in the application form for you and approve it.</u>

Anna        Oh, I didn't think of that. I'll need to go back and ask for it.

Mr. Stevenson        It shouldn't be a problem. Doctors in this town are used to providing them to support extension applications for students.

Anna        OK.

Mr. Stevenson        Now, are there any other problems about the essay?

Anna        Well, there are a few things. I'm still not sure about a good subject. I was looking at a couple of things and I found good resources on both of them. <u>My first idea was looking at how tax breaks offered by the Australian government can stimulate overseas investment.</u>

Mr. Stevenson        That sounds as though it has possibilities.

Anna        Yes, but it got rather over-complicated, as tax often is, apparently!

Mr. Stevenson        So what else have you thought about?

Anna        I was stuck for quite some time. I researched a lot in the library and online, but, as I said before, I found it hard to concentrate.

Page 175

Mr. Stevenson          You should have come to see me. I told you at the start that it was fine to get advice from me for choosing a topic.

Anna          I know. I just felt I should do it on my own. In the end, I looked at a historical overview of imports and exports between Australia and New Zealand. It would mean I would have to travel to New Zealand to check resources there, but my Dad said he'd pay for that. I also could avoid having to deal with tax, which would be a bonus!

Mr. Stevenson          That's certainly more straightforward, yet should also be academic enough to fulfill the requirements of the essay.

Anna          It is, but I found the subject rather boring. My first topic was more complex, but much more interesting.

Mr. Stevenson          Well, let's let the others go and we can discuss your topics now and make sure that you've chosen one by the end of our time.

Anna          OK. Thanks so much, Mr. Stevenson!

**That is the end of section three. You will now have half a minute to check your answers.**

*(30 second gap)*

**Now turn to section four.**

**Section four. You will hear a lecture on the signature. First you have some time to look at questions thirty-one to forty.**

*(50 second gap)*

**Now listen carefully and answer questions thirty-one to forty.**

Hello everyone. Today in this lecture we are going to look at the signature and how today the e-signature has developed.

In a culture of literacy and documentation, people obviously have always needed reliable ways to identify themselves and to be identified by others. This could be for creating charters, contracts or wills or for witnessing a document. Signing one's name by hand on paper has become the authoritative convention for this, and one that is closely aligned with our own sense of identity. In addition, signatures are important in legal documents, since by signing a paper document, the contents can become enforceable against the signatories.

The Sumerians, in the fifth to the third millennia BC, are considered the originators of writing, and these ancient people also developed ways of authenticating who wrote things. The Sumerians created seals, or intricate works of art carved in clay tablets, to identify possession. In many civilisations throughout history, people have used symbols and other marks to authenticate or acknowledge writings and drawings, and even to accept the contents of documents. The earliest actual handwriting signature we have has been traced to the year AD 439, and is attributed to the Roman Emperor Valentinian the Third.

Page 176

Signatures are connected with graphology, which is the study and analysis of handwriting especially in relation to human psychology. Graphology as a science originated in the mid sixteen hundreds when an Italian Professor, Camilo Baldi, wrote a book about how one can learn about a person's character and personality by looking at his writing. After the book was published, the study acquired a large following and spread widely. The Frenchman Jean Michon became the first to use the term "graphology", applying two Greek words to describe the new study: "grapho" meaning to write and "logos" meaning knowledge. Michon's contribution to graphology is immense. He formed graphological societies, published magazines and founded an academy for the subject. His approach was rather uncomplicated. He would study only the separate written elements, instead of a more complex approach. His method implied that presence of one graphological feature indicates a certain trait of character, whereas its absence implies the opposite feature. Not all his students and successors would accept Michon's method, though all agree that handwriting is a way of indicating personality. Wilheim Preyer, child psychologist, wrote in 1895 that writing originates in the brain, not in the fingers and that handwriting is actually brainwriting. This premise underlines how graphologists believe that a person's handwriting mirrors his or her thoughts.

Signatures were of particular interest to graphologists, but technology may now have made the handwritten signature obsolete. Technology companies in the 1980's and 1990's created instruments that let businesses send signed contracts across the globe in seconds. These technologies, now known as fax machines, email, and the World Wide Web, were considered major breakthroughs at the time. However, many people still questioned whether contracts that were signed and shared via fax, email, or Internet would hold up in court.

This led to what has become known as the electronic signature. In law, the one indispensable characteristic a signature has to possess is that it must physically add something to the document and that the signature will leave a physical mark or trace upon its surface. Electronic documents do not satisfy this condition, and the signature, like any alteration to an electronic document, does not leave a trace, or if it does, it is at such a microscopic level that it is in practice invisible. It looks nothing like the marks that have been accepted in law as constituting a hand-written signature.

In 1996, the United Nations looked into the topic of e-signatures and developed a framework with the purpose of encouraging e-commerce by providing a series of internationally acceptable rules. These rules removed many of the obstacles that had prevented foreign businesses from conducting electronic transactions in the past and ensured that electronic contracts would legally receive equal treatment to paper contracts going forward.

Many online businesses work with a click-to-agree basis, however, the desire for and utility of a handwritten, unique electronic signature is still apparent. Such a tool acts to enhance legal verification and adds a human touch to otherwise impersonal electronic documents and business deals. To fill this gap, lots of electronic signature software can now include options for the signer to provide a hand-drawn, personal electronic signature.

**That is the end of section four. You will now have half a minute to check your answers.**

*(30 second gap)*

**That is the end of listening test eight. In the IELTS test you would now have ten minutes to transfer your answers to the listening answer sheet.**

## LISTENING TEST 9 TRANSCRIPT

**This recording is copyright.**

**IELTS-Blog.com listening practice tests. Test nine. In the IELTS test you hear some recordings and you have to answer questions on them. You have time to read the instructions and questions and check your work. All recordings are played only once. The test is in four sections. Now turn to section one.**

**Section one. You will hear a conversation between a man and a woman at an employment agency.**

**First you have some time to look at questions one to five.**

*(20 second gap)*

**You will see that there is an example. This time only, the conversation relating to this will be played first.**

Sarah       Hi there. Welcome to People Central. I'm Sarah. How can I help you?

Mark        Hi Sarah. I'm Mark. I'm out of work right now and I'd like to find a job.

Sarah       I'm sure we can find something for you. We have lots of companies searching for people in different industries. What kind of job are you looking for?

Mark        I'm looking for a job in accountancy.

**So, accountancy is the correct answer.**

**Now the full test will begin. You should answer the questions as you listen, as the recording is not played twice. Listen carefully to the conversation and answer questions one to five.**

Sarah       Hi there. Welcome to People Central. I'm Sarah. How can I help you?

Mark        Hi Sarah. I'm Mark. I'm out of work right now and I'd like to find a job.

Sarah       I'm sure we can find something for you. We have lots of companies searching for people in different industries. What kind of job are you looking for?

Mark        I'm looking for a job in <u>accountancy</u>.

Sarah       Fine. I'm sure we can help you out with that. To begin with, I need to take some personal details for our files. You said your first name is Mark. What's your surname?

Mark        It's Castle. <u>C - A - S - T - L - E</u>.

Sarah       Thank you. And I need your address.

Mark        It's 13 Wellington Street, South Brisbane, Queensland.

Sarah       And the postcode?

Page 178

| Mark | It's four one oh one. |
|------|------|
| Sarah | Now I need your date of birth. |
| Mark | It's <u>thirtieth</u> of May, nineteen eighty-eight. |
| Sarah | Thank you. Let me just write that down. What was the month again? |
| Mark | May. The thirtieth of May, nineteen eighty-eight. |
| Sarah | Got it. Do you have an email address we can have? |
| Mark | Yes. Let me think for a second which is best. |
| Sarah | Do you have more than one? |
| Mark | Yes. I've got three. |
| Sarah | Really! |
| Mark | OK. I think I know. The address you can use is mark C at <u>australia</u> now dot com. |
| Sarah | OK. Just a minute. I have to write that all down. Did you say the provider is australia now dot com? |
| Mark | That's right. |
| Sarah | Good. Now, what contact phone numbers do you want to give me? |
| Mark | My home number is oh seven, three five five four, seven six seven one. |
| Sarah | Do you have a mobile phone number as well, as that's often the easiest way to get hold of people? |
| Mark | Of course. My mobile number is oh four six, nine one five three, <u>double four three</u>. |
| Sarah | Thanks. Now let me look at the form. Yes. There's just one more initial question left and that is whether you have any preferred areas where you'd like to work. |
| Mark | I don't really want to travel too far from home, so the area of Brisbane of course and I suppose anywhere within a drive of about <u>two hours</u>. |

**Before the conversation continues, you have some time to look at questions six to ten.**

*(20 second gap)*

**Now listen carefully and answer questions six to ten.**

| Sarah | Now, do you have your professional certificates? |
|------|------|
| Mark | Yes, here you are. They're all in this file. |

Sarah            I'll need to make some copies, but our copier is down. Do you mind if I keep them for a day?

Mark             I have <u>scans</u> of all of them. I can send them to you in a moment from my phone. You can just check the originals now.

Sarah            That's a good idea. I'll do that in a second. Now, we've got a selection of different companies looking for an accountant right now. Let's have a look at this first one. It's a big printing company down the coast called Gold Coast Printing. It's about an hour away and you can drive there quite easily.

Mark             I know that company. I can also get a <u>train</u> there quite easily, which I prefer, as it takes away the stress of the drive. I hate driving too far and buses are always too slow for me.

Sarah            Well, that's handy then. So, Gold Coast Printing needs someone full time, starting as soon as possible. The working hours are nine to five, Monday to Friday. For details about what exactly you'd be doing and the benefits package, you'll need to talk with the company itself. We just get you together.

Mark             It's certainly a possibility.

Sarah            I've another company here that needs a part-time accountant starting next month. They're an import export company and they have a Brisbane city centre location. Parking might be a problem, but the bus or tram would get you there easily.

Mark             Yes, the travel is no headache and it'd be fun to work in the city centre, but I'm not sure about a <u>part-time</u> job. I'll probably need to earn more than that can provide.

Sarah            Yes, that might be a problem. Let's look at this next one then. It's a fishing company called Barracuda down on the docks at the Brisbane River. They're a small family firm and they need a full-time accountant to help them with their expansion.

Mark             That would be very interesting, but I usually prefer larger companies. When it's a small company, there can often be problems with <u>personal relationships</u>.

Sarah            Well, that's the three possibilities that we have right now, though I know we might be getting some more next week.

Mark             Well, I was quite interested in Gold Coast Printing. I can get in contact with them and then see what comes in next week.

Sarah            OK. I'll set up a meeting for you with them.

Mark             By the way, do I need to pay you anything for placing me?

Sarah            The company who we place you with will pay us, but you aren't charged any <u>commission</u> at all.

Mark             Oh good. That's great for me.

**That is the end of section one. You will now have half a minute to check your answers.**

Page 180

*(30 second gap)*

**Now turn to section two.**

**Section two. You will hear a woman giving an introductory talk at a health centre open day. First you have some time to look at questions eleven to seventeen.**

*(20 second gap)*

**Now listen carefully to the information talk and answer questions eleven to seventeen.**

Welcome everyone today to the Sway Road Health Centre's Open Morning. My name is Lucy and I'm a nurse based at the Health Centre.

I'd first like to tell you a little about the health centre. We have six doctors who work here full-time and we are part of the district's medical services to those who live within our practice area. Currently, we have just in excess of <u>seven thousand</u> patients registered here. The patients are served from our centre here in Sway Road, but we also have a secondary centre in Church Road to ease congestion here and to make it easier for patients who live in that part of town.

To register with us, please come during opening hours, bringing a <u>photo ID</u>, a proof of residence address dated within three months of your application and your medical card, if you have one. If you don't, we'll ask you to fill out a registration form. We will ask for your preference for your doctor and we will try to comply, although this is not always possible. When applying, the reception staff will ask you for your medical history and they will also ask a nurse to take a <u>blood sample</u>. It's unusual that we would turn anyone down and you can see a doctor as soon as you've registered. Your updated medical card will be posted to you as soon as possible.

If you want to make an appointment with us, this should be made by telephone and not by <u>email</u>. We have email, but due to the large amount we receive, some do not get read fast enough and appointments are not made in time. Calls can be made to our centre during our opening hours, which are <u>eight</u> a.m. to one p.m. and two p.m. to seven p.m. Monday to Friday. Between one and two p.m., the centre is closed, except for emergency calls only. We are closed on Saturdays, Sundays and on <u>public holidays</u>. If you do have an emergency, we would stress that a serious one would be better served by going to hospital or by calling an ambulance.

Our practice supports the training of medical students and you might be asked whether your visit to a nurse or doctor can be done with a student present. There is no obligation for you to accept this and the student will not be present if you prefer to have your consultation in private.

Our surgery offers a complete travel service, including a full range of vaccinations. The wide diversity of destinations and the increased popularity of adventure holidays increase the risk to your health, which in turn makes the service we provide increasingly complex. Ask for a <u>travel risk form</u> at Reception or download it from our website and hand it in to our Reception as soon as you've booked your holiday. Our nurse will review the form and advise you on the vaccinations you should have. It's also a good idea to keep a vaccination card, so you have a record of what you have had over the years. Vaccinations must be paid for on the day of administration, unless you are covered by a health insurer.

**You now have some time to look at questions eighteen to twenty.**

*(20 second gap)*

**Now listen to the rest of the introductory talk and answer questions eighteen to twenty.**

Finally, if you have any suggestions to improve our service, please use the suggestion box <u>at Reception</u>. We will provide you with paper and pen if you don't have any. Also, from time to time, people feel that they have a problem with their care. If you have any complaints about the service you receive at our health centre, please bring this to the attention of the <u>practice manager,</u> who will be happy to discuss the issue. We have a complaints procedure that is available at Reception or it can be downloaded from our website.

So, today, all our staff are here for this Saturday morning, so that you can look around the centre and ask any questions. This includes all our doctors, nurses and support staff. All the areas are open, except for the <u>practice offices</u>, which have some sensitive material. You can wander around and ask anyone questions, though please remember that the doctors are not here for consultations, so please do not turn any conversations into a doctor's visit.

That's enough from me. Please now look around and ask whatever questions you want. If you'd like to register today, then just go to Reception and they'll get you organised. I'll be based here in the waiting room, so you can ask me any questions as well of course.

**That is the end of section two. You will now have half a minute to check your answers.**

*(30 second gap)*

**Now turn to section three.**

**Section three. You will hear a man and a woman discussing the man's recent training. First you have some time to look at questions twenty-one to twenty-five.**

*(20 second gap)*

**Now listen carefully and answer questions twenty-one to twenty-five.**

| Christine | Hi Kevin. Welcome back. |
|---|---|
| Kevin | Hi Christine. Thanks. It's good to be back. |
| Christine | Do you have a moment? I want to get some feedback about the training you've been on. |
| Kevin | Of course. I have a meeting in twenty minutes, but I'm free until then. |
| Christine | So, you were away for three nights. Was the accommodation OK? |
| Kevin | <u>Well, the room was clean and it was serviced every day before I got back. It was a little bit noisy, as the side of the hotel where I was sleeping was quite near a train line, so every time a train passed, I could hear it quite clearly. Trains weren't that common at night though, so it didn't disturb me too much.</u> |

**Christine**      I see. Well, next time we book that hotel, we'll request a room away from that side. Did you find the conference centre where the training was easily?

**Kevin**      The directions they gave me were atrocious. I ended up being half an hour late on the first day. The directions instructed me to take a road that went the other way. It was only when I stopped at a petrol station and asked for directions that I was able to get back on the right road.

**Christine**      Didn't you have a SATNAV?

**Kevin**      I did, but the charging cable had broken and it wasn't working that morning. If it had been working, then there would have been no trouble at all.

**Christine**      Were they OK that you were so late on the first day?

**Kevin**      Some of the other trainees gave me looks, but the trainer wasn't worried and she was very apologetic about the problems. She even phoned her boss to complain at the first break and told me they would fix things immediately.

**Christine**      That's more like it.

**Kevin**      Yes, and that really summed up the trainer. Nothing was too much trouble for her. She was also extremely knowledgeable about her subject and skilled at getting her ideas across. A natural teacher, I'd say.

**Christine**      I'm happy about that. At my last training, the trainer was just awful. He was late, he hadn't prepared and he plainly didn't care about any of the trainees.

**Kevin**      That does sound awful.

**Christine**      Was everything OK at the conference centre?

**Kevin**      Well, the Internet connection was a bit slow, which was annoying, as I wanted to keep in contact with the office. It didn't really affect the software training though, as we didn't need to go online very often. The training room had everything that was needed, though it would have been nice to have drinks there. These places are all air-conditioned and it can make you very dry. The food was fine and the place was clean and tidy.

**Christine**      How were the other trainees?

**Kevin**      Well, I got a bit of a frosty reception when I first arrived, because of my lateness, but they soon warmed up after they heard the reasons and were fantastic. We all became very friendly.

**Christine**      Did you all have the same knowledge level?

**Kevin**      Yes, pretty much. It was really good in that way, as we all shared the same problems and so we could discuss things and learn from each other. It was actually really productive and the best part of the training. We swapped contact details, so that we can keep in touch and help each other with the new software installations.

**Christine**      It's often the way that contacts can be just as productive as the training.

| | |
|---|---|
| Kevin | Yes. Exactly. |

**You now have some time to look at questions twenty-six to thirty.**

*(20 second gap)*

**Now listen to the rest of the discussion and answer questions twenty-six to thirty.**

| | |
|---|---|
| Christine | So, did you manage to get the software all installed on our systems? |
| Kevin | Yes, I did, but it was quite a struggle. |
| Christine | What happened? |
| Kevin | The plan was after the training, <u>I would spend the weekend here at the offices installing everything.</u> |
| Christine | <u>That was a bit tough, having to spend the weekend here.</u> |
| Kevin | <u>Yes, but when things like this happen, my contract states that I get an extra four days in lieu that I can add to my summer holiday.</u> That made my wife quite happy. |
| Christine | I bet it did. |
| Kevin | So, I had a real long session here at the weekend. |
| Christine | What happened? |
| Kevin | The first thing was that <u>our existing operating system was a bit out of date for the new software. In order to fix that, I had to run updates on the whole system and during that time, I just had to wait.</u> |
| Christine | Did it take long? |
| Kevin | A couple of hours. It had to be done though, or I'd have had to buy new computers for everyone. The updates were slow, but free! <u>The next problem was that our systems just couldn't accept the new software. I tried everything, but it wouldn't work. I thought I'd have to get a consultant in this morning to help me.</u> |
| Christine | <u>How did you fix that in the end?</u> |
| Kevin | <u>Fortunately, one of my fellow trainees on the course had just done what I was trying to do, so I called her. She managed to talk me through everything.</u> It took a bit of time though, and I really thought I'd have to get the consultants in. |
| Christine | So it all got installed in the end? |
| Kevin | Yes, but the problems hadn't ended. |
| Christine | What happened next? |
| Kevin | Well, after I got everything fixed up, I did a few trial runs in order to see if things were working well. It seemed fine, but then I noticed some irregularities. <u>Unfortunately, a bug had got into the system and was starting to mess things up.</u> |

Page 184

Christine       How did you fix that?

Kevin       It was lucky I saw it so early or I'd never have fixed it. I had a look at the code that was causing the problem and I recognised it. It was something the antivirus set-up we have already couldn't handle, so I had to buy some more complex add-ons. They were downloaded straight away and they cleared away the bug.

Christine       Was that the end of it?

Kevin       Almost. The last thing was that I stayed so long at the office on Sunday night that the automatic alarm was set while I was still there. Of course, the alarm went off and the alarm was blaring out. I thought the police were going to come and take me away.

Christine       Did you call the security firm and give them the all-clear password?

Kevin       Yes, I did, but it was the old one. I gave the new one straight away afterwards, but it was too late then. I had to call the boss and he called the security. Luckily, it all happened before the police got there.

**That is the end of section three. You will now have half a minute to check your answers.**

*(30 second gap)*

**Now turn to section four.**

**Section four. You will hear a lecture on the Atacama Desert in Chile. First you have some time to look at questions thirty-one to forty.**

*(50 second gap)*

**Now listen carefully and answer questions thirty-one to forty.**

Good morning everyone and welcome to this lecture on geography. We are going to continue our focus on deserts and desertification and today, we'll look at the phenomenon of rain shadow deserts. As an example, we'll have a look at the Atacama Desert, the highest and driest desert in the world.

The centre of the Atacama Desert is known as the driest place on Earth. The reason for the Atacama's aridity is due to its special geographical conditions, which create what is known as a rain shadow over the area. Rain shadow deserts are formed because tall mountain ranges prevent moisture-rich clouds from reaching areas on the other side of the range. In the case of the Atacama Desert, winds coming off the Atlantic Ocean carry moisture towards the Andes. The mountains cause the moist air to rise until condensation causes the moisture to be released as rain. As all this moisture is released from the cloud, only dry air moves over the top of the Andes. Any wind that comes off the Pacific towards the Atacama Desert is too cool to retain any moisture. The result is that nearly all the air above the Atacama is too dry to create any rain and it is this that is known as a rain shadow.

One unexpected benefit of the rain shadow over the Atacama and the desert's high altitude is that it creates an unusually clear sky and so the area is ideal for the observation of space. Last year, the US National Science Foundation inaugurated the Atacama Large Millimetre Array, one of the world's most powerful telescopes. The telescope comprises sixty-six antennas that will provide high-resolution images

Page 185

of the earliest galaxies in the distant universe, as well as the <u>formation processes</u> of planets circling stars in our own Milky Way galaxy. Scientists from around the world will have the opportunity to explore such objects as they never could before, with an array of telescopes more than a hundred times more powerful than any previous millimetre arrays.

The Atacama Desert of Chile covers the northern third of the country, stretching more than a thousand kilometres. Straddling the southern border of Peru, it is bound on the west by <u>barren hills</u> on the Pacific coast, and it extends east into the Andes Mountains. At an average elevation of about four thousand metres, it is not only the highest desert in the world, but also one of the coldest, with temperatures averaging between zero and minus twenty-five degrees Celsius.

The plant and animal life in the Atacama survive under perhaps the Earth's most demanding conditions. Local populations have relied on some of the species of plant for <u>medical purposes</u> for generations. Animal life is very rare in this desert, though there are a few insects and lizards to be found. Mice and foxes are also present, but in very small numbers.

In spite of its inhospitable environment, the Atacama Desert has a variety of natural resources and the Atacama was one of Chile's chief sources of wealth until the First World War. Prior to that time, that nation had a <u>monopoly</u> on the nitrate commerce worldwide. Three million tons were extracted in some years and the taxes alone on these exports amounted to fifty per cent of the government's revenues. Currently, the Atacama Desert is littered with approximately one hundred and seventy abandoned nitrate mining towns, almost all of which were shut down decades after the invention of synthetic nitrate in Germany at the turn of the twentieth century. Since that time, sulphur has been mined, as well as copper, which is the region's chief source of revenue, providing over thirty per cent of the world's <u>copper</u> supply. The Atacama border dispute between Chile and Bolivia began in the eighteen hundreds over these resources.

Because of the lack of rainfall, the environment offers little support to agriculture, but some farming is done near the river oases. Lemons are grown on the shores of the salt marshes, while potatoes and alfalfa are grown near the Loa River.

Despite extremes and desolation, there is stunning beauty and tourism is now one of the major sources of income for the area. With the Andes as a backdrop, the desert contains five snow-topped volcanoes, which are the highest volcanoes in the world. The desert also has impressive geysers, lagoons and other spectacular natural features. In addition, these beautiful and rare sites draw <u>scientists</u> wishing to study the area and, as a result, environmentalists are concerned about the number of people who enter the Atacama and the environmentalists claim that the visitors have not been educated sufficiently to understand the <u>delicate balance</u> that is needed in this environment. Urbanisation and mining operations have already brought about some damage, and overgrazing of domestic livestock has occurred in the north, as has commercial gathering of rare plants, including cacti and bulbs. It's hard enough for plants to grow in this area as it is, without having their <u>growth cycles</u> broken up by humans.

**That is the end of section four. You will now have half a minute to check your answers.**

*(30 second gap)*

**That is the end of listening test nine. In the IELTS test you would now have ten minutes to transfer your answers to the listening answer sheet.**

## LISTENING TEST 10 TRANSCRIPT

**This recording is copyright.**

**IELTS-Blog.com listening practice tests. Test ten. In the IELTS test you hear some recordings and you have to answer questions on them. You have time to read the instructions and questions and check your work. All recordings are played only once. The test is in four sections. Now turn to section one.**

**Section one. You will hear a conversation between a man and a woman at an estate agency.**

**First you have some time to look at questions one to five.**

*(20 second gap)*

**You will see that there is an example. This time only, the conversation relating to this will be played first.**

Charlotte      Hello, my name's Charlotte. I'm moving to this area in two months and I was hoping that you would be able to help me with finding somewhere to live.

Matthew      Good morning, Charlotte. I'm Matthew. Welcome to Anglian Estates. I'm sure we'll be able to help you. Were you looking to buy or rent a place to live?

Charlotte      Just somewhere to rent.

Matthew      And in which post code would you like to live?

Charlotte      My preferred one is AE5.

**So, AE5 is the correct answer.**

**Now the full test will begin. You should answer the questions as you listen, as the recording is not played twice. Listen carefully to the conversation and answer questions one to five.**

Charlotte      Hello, my name's Charlotte. I'm moving to this area in two months and I was hoping that you would be able to help me with finding somewhere to live.

Matthew      Good morning, Charlotte. I'm Matthew. Welcome to Anglian Estates. I'm sure we'll be able to help you. Were you looking to buy or rent a place to live?

Charlotte      Just somewhere to rent.

Matthew      And in which post code would you like to live?

Charlotte      My preferred one is AE5.

Matthew      What kind of place were you thinking of, Charlotte? A house, an apartment, a flat, a studio?

Charlotte      I'd eventually be looking for a house, but to start with, just a small apartment will be fine.

Matthew      How large an apartment would you need?

**Charlotte**   It's for my daughter and I only and we'll need a bedroom each, so we'll need <u>two</u> of them. I'd also want a separate bathroom and kitchen and a living room, of course.

**Matthew**   OK. I'll just write that down.

**Charlotte**   Do you know of many apartments like I've described?

**Matthew**   Yes, I think so. We have quite a number of apartments on our books right now. Most of them fit your description, as that's what people are looking for nowadays.

**Charlotte**   Oh good.

**Matthew**   Now, what's your rental budget?

**Charlotte**   <u>A thousand dollars</u> a week.

**Matthew**   That's good. You should be able to find something nice for that. Is there anything else particular about the apartment you want?

**Charlotte**   First of all, I need the apartment near my daughter's school.

**Matthew**   What's the name of the school?

**Charlotte**   It's called St. Mary's.

**Matthew**   Oh yes. I know it. It's in Talbot Avenue.

**Charlotte**   That's right. I'd also like the apartment semi-furnished, please.

**Matthew**   Including what exactly?

**Charlotte**   The bedrooms and living room can be empty, but I'd like all the basics in <u>the kitchen</u>, like a cooker, fridge-freezer and washing machine.

**Matthew**   Yes, I know what you mean. Don't worry. In our apartments, we always have all those basic things you need included in the rental.

**Charlotte**   Good. It would be nice to have a garden, as well, although I know that's not so common with apartments.

**Matthew**   Well, we have some ground floor apartments that have gardens accompanying the rental. We can look at some of those. The only issue there is that those apartments specify that you'll need to be accountable for <u>the garden's maintenance</u>. Would that be OK?

**Charlotte**   That's fine. I have green fingers!

**Matthew**   Anything else?

**Charlotte**   I don't think so.

**Matthew**   I'll just tell you a little about our terms and conditions. Before we show you any details, we'll ask you to sign a contract. This does not commit you to only working with us or anything, but it does specify that any apartments that you are shown by us, you have to rent through us.

Charlotte　　　That seems fair enough.

Matthew　　　The contract also lays out our commission structure. This basically means that you have to pay <u>two months' rent</u> to us if you decide to rent an apartment shown to you by us.

Charlotte　　　That all seems in order.

Matthew　　　Good.

**Before the conversation continues, you have some time to look at questions six to ten.**

*(20 second gap)*

**Now listen carefully and answer questions six to ten.**

Matthew　　　So, let's see what we have that fits your requirements. To start with, there's a nice place in Grantham Gardens.

Charlotte　　　I'll just get my pen to make some notes. Here it is. Off you go.

Matthew　　　So, this apartment is on the first floor. It's just been <u>renovated</u> and has the number of rooms you specified. It has no garden unfortunately, but it does have a nice balcony that comes out of the living room and looks out over the nearby park.

Charlotte　　　That seems very nice. Is it close to Georgina's school?

Matthew　　　Oh yes. I reckon it would be a ten-minute walk from St. Mary's.

Charlotte　　　That's a big advantage if she can walk to school herself. That would really free me up.

Matthew　　　It also fits with your budget, although the <u>deposit</u> is quite high. Hopefully, you'd get that
back though.

Charlotte　　　I hope so. Do you have any others, Matthew?

Matthew　　　Oh yes. I've a couple more right here and I should be able to show you some details of the others this afternoon. I can send the details by emails if we don't have time today.

Charlotte　　　OK. I'll give you my email address at the end.

Matthew　　　Now the second apartment is in Lawrence Close. This is a ground floor flat, so you can walk out into the garden from the <u>living room</u>. The garden is around one hundred and fifty square metres, so it's not enormous, but not too small either.

Charlotte　　　That sounds about right.

Matthew　　　Good. Now the number of rooms is fine, but a drawback is that it's not so close to St. Mary's. It would be too long for your daughter to walk.

Charlotte　　　I could drive her if the apartment was what we wanted.

Matthew　　　She could also take the <u>school bus</u>, which leaves at the top of the road. It's not as convenient, but it's an advantage. Something else I like about this apartment is the wooden floors. They're very nicely laid and they look beautiful.

| Charlotte | That sounds very nice. I'll have to see it. Is it within my budget? |
|---|---|
| Matthew | It's a little bit over, but not by much. |
| Charlotte | That should be fine. |

Matthew    The last apartment that I want to tell you about right now is in Greene Road. This is again a nice apartment and is in line with your budget. It has the right number of rooms and it's walking distance from your daughter's school. It's on the third floor of a purpose-built building, but there is an elevator and each flat has an allocated section of the large garden.

Charlotte    Hmm. I'm not sure about the third floor.

Matthew    Another drawback is that the kitchen and living room are <u>combined</u> and you wanted them separated. I have to say though, it's done very nicely and the building is modern and immaculately looked after.

Charlotte    It's worth looking at then?

Matthew    Oh yes. I think you'll quite like it in spite of this first impression.

**That is the end of section one. You will now have half a minute to check your answers.**

*(30 second gap)*

**Now turn to section two.**

**Section two. You will hear a woman giving a talk on the radio about a new citizens advice office. First you have some time to look at questions eleven to fifteen.**

*(20 second gap)*

**Now listen carefully to the talk and answer questions eleven to fifteen.**

Presenter    Good morning everyone and welcome back to Radio GTFM. You may have heard recently that the town is getting a new citizens advice office and Annette Arnold is here today to tell us a little about it. Welcome, Annette.

Annette    Thank you for having me on the show. So, yes, the town finally has a citizens advice office. The people who live in our town can come and get free, confidential and impartial guidance on all aspects of their lives. We can be found right in the centre of the town in the square, where you'll find the town hall, the old post office, the National Credit Bank, the main town police station, the tourist information office, the main town church, Boodles Department store and the art gallery. <u>We're in the building that used to be the square's post office and, as you come out of the front of our building into the square, on our right is the tourist information office</u> and on our left is the National Credit Bank. You can't miss our entrance. We have painted the whole of our front door bright yellow and the rest of the building's front is a rather loud shade of green. You can't miss all that! <u>Directly opposite from our building is the town hall.</u>

People come to offices like ours for all sorts of advice. To give you an example, the world of work is where we can often help the people who visit us. This can cover all sorts of things. We can't actually help you find a job, but we can help with problems at work. <u>This can range from grievances and pay to vacation</u>

Page 190

entitlements and discrimination. Having a job is an essential part of most people's lives and you can be faced with many difficult issues, so it is essential to know what you should do.

Another common area is to do with money. If you find that you owe money to organisations or people, we can look at your options and provide guidance on how to deal with your problem. Not many things can cause more stress than this and it's important to address it before things get out of hand. We can't lend you the money ourselves, but we have contacts in banking and government that can help.

Another popular area is tax. Everyone finds this a complex area and at some time everyone needs advice on it. We can show you how to work out whether you need to pay income tax and how it's collected. We can also tell you if you've paid too much tax and there are guides to council tax and inheritance tax. We're not allowed to recommend any accountants to you, but you can research that on the Internet if you feel you need someone after us to do any tax related work.

**You now have some time to look at questions sixteen to twenty.**

*(20 second gap)*

**Now listen to the rest of the talk and answer questions sixteen to twenty.**

So, we've had a number of emails asking where the different sections are within our building. Of course, there is a sign up at the entrance of the building to help you and all the information is on our website.

I didn't mention it earlier, but we have a big section on education. This office can help you with all your enquiries on your and your children's education. This is found on the first floor in room twenty-five and the secretary there, Mrs. Atkins, will help you get started.

Another office I didn't mention earlier is the one for relationships, which is also on the first floor in room twenty-nine. This place can give you advice on keeping your relationship together through therapy and it can also advise you on your rights within the law if your relationship breaks down.

We don't have a money office for you to pay any bills, as all our advice is for free. We do, however, welcome any donations you might want to give us. Although the government funds us to some extent, money's tight nowadays and we're always short at the end of the year. If you'd like to offer us any funds, please speak to the receptionist on the ground floor and she will direct you to whichever manager is on duty at that time. The money advice office is next to reception in room one, but don't go there for donations and don't go there for government benefits.

The office for any enquiries relating to employment is in room two on the ground floor opposite reception. They will help you with advice on all your rights and how to solve problems. One word of advice about this office is that they are often very busy, as their advice is very popular. Don't be too disappointed if someone can't see you right away. They may have to make an appointment for you to come back at another time, but you won't have to wait too long. Next to room two are the bathrooms, and the next one, room four, is our section on benefits. This office will help you with all questions to do with your rights to money from the government.

Also on the ground floor, you can find our offices on discrimination. This is found in room nine. Here you can get advice if you think you've been treated differently because of who you are. Please note that this does not include employment in our offices. You need to go to the employment office for that.

Room eighteen on the first floor is the office for our consumer section. When you buy goods or services, the law gives you consumer rights. These protect you from being treated unfairly by a trader. You may have received poor service or you may want to switch energy suppliers or cancel a contract. You can also learn more about what you can expect to find in a consumer contract.

**That is the end of section two. You will now have half a minute to check your answers.**

*(30 second gap)*

**Now turn to section three.**

**Section three. You will hear two students giving a presentation to their teacher. First you have some time to look at questions twenty-one to twenty-five.**

*(20 second gap)*

**Now listen carefully and answer questions twenty-one to twenty-five.**

Dr. Cork       Hello, everyone. So, in today's seminar, we're going to be listening to a short presentation. That's you, Roger, and your partner, Josie.

Roger       That's right, Doctor Cork.

Dr. Cork       So, what are you going to talk about?

Josie       We had some problems choosing a topic actually.

Dr. Cork       I thought you both wanted to examine the effects of the invention of the aerosol spray?

Roger       That was our first idea, but the problem was that we found there was a group in the other class who wanted to do that too.

Josie       Also, today's application of the invention seemed too much linked to its influence on the painting industry and we looked at that a few weeks ago.

Dr. Cork       I see. Yes, I think you were wise to steer clear of that. What other ideas did you have?

Josie       We were stuck for a good topic for some time. In the end, Roger had some reasonable ideas.

Roger       Thanks, Josie. So, one idea was that we could look into how the industrial revolution was affected by the invention of the spinning machine. This invention revolutionised the garment manufacturing industry and led to the loss of many jobs in factories.

Dr. Cork       That seems like a good project.

Josie       Yes, we thought so too, but it was hard finding the right sources.

Dr. Cork       I thought there would be plenty on that.

Josie          So did we, but the library had very little. We then had a look at a couple of other inventions, for example Volta's invention of the chemical battery. Although this happened a long time ago, and we wanted to link it to the development of the mobile phone and how its development depended largely on getting a battery small enough to make them portable.

Dr. Cork        That might be too big a time between the invention and its effect.

Roger          We came to that conclusion too, though it's a shame, as it was such an interesting topic.

Dr. Cork        What came next?

Roger          We looked at how the sextant was invented, which was interesting, as it was invented in the US and the UK simultaneously. By measuring angular distances between objects, people were able to work out their geographical position relative to celestial objects. This allowed ships at sea to be able to work out their positions reasonably accurately and no doubt saved thousands of lives.

Dr. Cork        Was there a problem with that topic?

Josie          We thought so. The effect of the invention was so long ago that we thought it was no longer very relevant.

Dr. Cork        I see what you mean. You'd probably have been alright though.

Roger          We decided not to take a chance.

Dr. Cork        Well, it's often good to play safe.

Roger          I then wanted to look at the invention of modern light polarisers, which were created by the American physicist, Edward Land.

Dr. Cork        What do they do?

Josie          They eliminate glare and were used in the first instant cameras.

Dr. Cork        And what was wrong with that?

Josie          That was my fault, I'm afraid. I just found that topic really boring.

Roger          I didn't want to force her, so we finally just chose a different subject.

**You now have some time to look at questions twenty-six to thirty.**

*(20 second gap)*

**Now listen to the rest of the presentation and answer questions twenty-six to thirty.**

Dr. Cork        So, what did you finally decide on to talk about today?

Josie          We chose the invention of the ballpoint pen.

Dr. Cork        Off you go then.

Roger        I'm starting. So, like many inventions, the ballpoint pen came from a need and this need for a different type of pen came about because of ink. Traditional fountain pens used an ink that dried too slowly. Quick-drying ink was available, as it was used in the printing business. This ink was soft and acidic as was needed, but it was not suitable for pens, it as it was too thick to pass through the nib of the traditional pen.

Dr. Cork        Am I right in saying that the ballpoint pen was invented by a Hungarian?

Josie        That's right. In the early 1930's, Lazlo Biro, a Hungarian journalist, thought about how printing ink could be used in a pen. Biro's idea was to fit a tiny metal ball bearing at the end of the pen. This was not a new idea. In 1888, the American John Loud patented a roller-ball-tip marking pen. Loud invented his pen, which had a reservoir of ink and a roller ball, in order to apply thick ink to leather hides. Loud's pen was never produced, and neither were three hundred and fifty other patented designs for ball point pens over the next thirty years. The problem was the ink, if it was too thin the pen leaked, if it was too thick, the pen clogged, and sometimes it did both.

Dr. Cork        So, Biro's was the first ballpoint pen commercially successful?

Roger        That's right, but not in Hungary. Biro had to leave Hungary just before the start of Word War Two and he created a new home for himself in Argentina. There, Biro set up a business producing his new pens, which were later also manufactured under licence in the UK and the US.

Josie        Biro's original design is still the one that's used by most big manufacturers of pens. In fact, the Biro company has problems with people using the word, Biro. Because the Biro pen has been so successful, people often use it as a generic term rather than as a trade name.

Dr. Cork        So, how did Biro's ballpoint pen work?

Roger        At the bottom or point of the pen is a small ball bearing, from which the name ballpoint comes. Above the ball bearing is a channel for the ink to flow down, known as the ink tube. In the middle of the ink tube is a central spring.

Dr. Cork        It already sounds complicated. Is this the process that is used in the cheap ballpoint pen nowadays?

Roger        It does sound complicated, but it isn't really. And yes. All modern ballpoint pens use this process.

Dr. Cork        Really! Anyway, please carry on.

Roger        The idea is that the pen is pressed down onto the paper when writing. This action forces the spring to rise, so that its top section lifts and allows a gap to open between the ink tube and the ink tank, which is found above the spring in the body of the pen. The ink can then flow down to the ball bearing, coating it, as the ball bearing revolves during the writing process. In this way, quick-drying ink was able to be used in what was called the ballpoint pen.

Dr. Cork        That's very interesting. Now, let's hear your section on the effects of this invention.

**That is the end of section three. You will now have half a minute to check your answers.**

*(30 second gap)*

**Now turn to section four.**

**Section four. You will hear a lecture on rice. First you have some time to look at questions thirty-one to forty.**

*(50 second gap)*

**Now listen carefully and answer questions thirty-one to forty.**

Hello everyone. Today in this agriculture lecture, we are going to take a look at one of the world's great staples, especially in Asia. It's also the third highest produced agricultural plant produced globally after sugarcane and maize.

While rice has featured in the agriculture of South and East Asia since prehistoric times, recent archaeological research has offered new insights and raised new questions about when, how and why rice first came to be cultivated. The highly productive rice crops of today are adapted plants, which differ in genetics from wild rice by possessing adaptations that make them productive in cultivation, but also dependent on cultivation for survival.

It has long appeared that rice agriculture began in South-central China, somewhere along the Yangzte river, and spread from there southwards and to northeast towards Korea and Japan. However, archaeologists working in India have argued that their evidence suggests an origin of rice cultivation in the Ganges river valley. For both regions, there are current controversies about how early rice was domesticated as opposed to being gathered wild. It seems that the origins of rice will remain in obscurity and whatever claims have been made cannot really be substantiated. More relevant for us is looking at how good rice is grown in quantities to sustain human populations.

In spite of its widespread use, rice requires special cultivation and care. The first is seed selection. This is important, as different cultivation environments require different strains of rice in order to ensure that the highest possible yields are achieved. This does not usually need to be done by individual farmers. Nowadays, agricultural ministries have picked the optimum seeds for all the varying environments in their countries. The appropriate seeds are in turn made available to the appropriate areas. Next, as in other types of agriculture, the preparation of the land where the rice will be grown is important to create soil where the best possible root systems can be created and retained. If these are well-established, the rice plant should develop to a good size and in turn produce a good return of rice.

Once the land is ready, the plants can be introduced. The two main methods used for introducing rice plants to the soil are transplanting and direct seeding, and the choice between the two usually depends on the type of fields into which the rice will be put. Transplanting is the more popular plant establishment technique in much of Asia. It occurs when pre-germinated seedlings from a nursery are transferred from a seedbed to the wet field. Direct seeding is when dry seed or pre-germinated seeds and seedlings are sown by hand or planted by machine in the field.

One of the key areas of rice agriculture is water management. Cultivated rice is extremely sensitive to water shortages and when the soil water content drops below saturation, most rice varieties develop symptoms of water stress. Good water management practices are therefore needed to maximise rice yield. Nutrient management is another key area. Farmers must ensure that rice plants get the proper nutrients at the right time. Prolonged flooding of where the rice is grown ensures that farmers are able to conserve soil organic matter and also ensures that the rice receives free input of nitrogen from biological sources. Rice crops also require constant health administration, as the rice plant can come under threat from different sources in the field. A good understanding of <u>pest</u> management is required.

When the rice plants are ready, they need to be harvested carefully. Depending on the variety, a rice crop usually reaches maturity at around one hundred and twenty days after crop establishment. Good harvesting methods help maximise grain yield and minimise grain damage and deterioration. Mechanical harvesting using reapers or combine harvesters is the other option, but is not so common due to the poor <u>availability</u> and cost of machinery. Manual harvesting is popular across Asia and involves cutting the rice crop with simple hand tools like sickles and knives. Manual harvesting usually requires forty to eighty man-hours per hectare and it takes additional labour to manually collect and haul the harvested crop.

After harvest, the rice grain undergoes a number of processes, depending on how it will be used. <u>Drying</u> is the process that reduces grain moisture content to a safe level for storage and it is the most critical operation after harvesting a rice crop. Delays in this or doing it badly will reduce grain quality and result in post harvest losses. The correct storage conditions will ensure minimal loss of rice due to changes in weather and moisture content, rodents, insects and microorganisms. Finally, the milling of rice is a crucial post-production step. The basic objective of a rice milling system is to remove the husk and the bran layers and to produce an edible, white or brown rice kernel that is sufficiently milled and free of impurities.

**That is the end of section four. You will now have half a minute to check your answers.**

*(30 second gap)*

**That is the end of listening test ten. In the IELTS test you would now have ten minutes to transfer your answers to the listening answer sheet.**

CPSIA information can be obtained
at www.ICGtesting.com
Printed in the USA
LVOW09s1629280917
550415LV00008B/485/P